BANK LIKE A BOSS

How Entrepreneurs Maintain Access to Cash In Good Times and Bad

By Richard Barbercheck

STRATEGIC
ORIENTATION

NAVIGATION FOR YOUR BUSINESS

BANK LIKE A BOSS: HOW ENTREPRENEURS MAINTAIN ACCESS TO CASH IN GOOD TIMES AND BAD

Strategic Orientation Publishing / 2021
Copyright © 2021 by Richard Barbercheck

Note: Cover art and graphics by Christen Barbercheck

ISBN: 978-0-578-88075-4
Printed in the United States of America

Find out more at StrategicOrientation.com.

Dedication

This book is dedicated first, to my loving wife Teresa, who has been by my side supporting all my efforts to grow a worthwhile career, be a loving husband and father, and a better version of myself.

It is further dedicated to all those who made me who I am today. Those who mentored and taught me, often without knowing, through the shear experience of personal and professional interaction. None of us succeed on our own, and I have been blessed with many successes, all of which should be credited to the employers, colleagues, friends, family, business owners, and others that influenced me along the way.

Thank you for the guidance.
It is valuable and appreciated.
May this book be one small way of giving
back for that which has been given.

Acknowledgements

Authors get the privilege of having their name on the cover, but there isn't a book written that hasn't required the assistance, insight, or guidance from others.
It is with my sincere appreciation that I acknowledge:

Dan Barbercheck, President / ECD, Red7e for assisting with the title creation and content review.

Christen Barbercheck, for assisting with the interior graphics, cover design, and content review.

Shannon Miller, for assisting with content review and final proofreading.

"Today, small to midsized firms are navigating a fast moving business environment that requires agility, discipline and forward thinking to survive and thrive. Richard Barbercheck masterfully blends his vast banking and business consulting experiences to provide a well-balanced, multi-disciplinary view on managing critical financial resources. *Bank Like A Boss* is an insightful field book for business owners responsible to maintain and expand bank financing and support for long-term success."

Richard Flynn, CPA, President/CEO & Founder
Flynn & Company, Inc.

"*Bank Like A Boss* is like the Rosetta Stone for Bankers and Business Owners. A must read for all bankers and borrowers. It easily translates banking language into borrower language while informing the reader of actions that make their business bankable. I have read so many books on banking and I honestly think this might be the best one I have ever read. Simple but detailed, from the perspective of the bank and the borrower."

Brian Dunlap, President/CEO
RiverHills Bank

"*Bank Like A Boss* presents a practical view for business owners and managers of the significance of assuring their business has access to the cash they need in good times and bad. Importantly, Richard Barbercheck provides a 360° view of the vital role Cash plays in the viability and success of any business. Richard blends his skill, knowledge and experience as a business owner, banking professional, and senior bank executive, into solid guidance for business owners challenged by business continuity and sustainability."

Andy McCreanor, CEO
Access Business Finance, Inc.
An SBA Certified Development Company

"Bank Like A Boss: How Entrepreneurs Maintain Access to Cash in Good Times and Bad, is an excellent synopsis of how every business owner and manager should think about their banking relationships. Richard uses his three plus decades of experience in business, banking, coaching, and consulting to provide a realistic view of the phases a business experiences and how that impacts the financial management of a company. A business owner can use this book as a "how to" in managing bankability over the long-term management of their business."

Claude Davis
Managing Director, Brixey and Meyer Capital
Board Chairman, First Financial Bancorp

"Bank Like A Boss is a must read for any entrepreneur starting a business. Cash is King, access to credit, and your availability to get credit is critical to staying in business. *Bank like A Boss* will walk you through the business life cycles as a source of cash. If you start a business, your attitude must be to never quit, even when you get kicked in the teeth. Banking plus cash liquidity is a large part of it."

Michael Gates, Developer

"Bank Like A Boss is an owner's manual for small business owners. Full of actionable items in layperson's terms, it is intended to eliminate unknowns and increase a small business' ability to survive and thrive. Richard Barbercheck's simple explanation of the five C's of credit alone is worth the read. These are not rocket science, so a more common understanding of these basic business concepts provides a clear recipe for yielding a fruitful borrower/lender relationship built on trust."

Michael J. Adelman, President & CEO
Ohio Banker's League

"Richard Barbercheck has written a delightful guide for business owners seeking to establish and maintain constructive, long-lasting relationships with their bankers. *Bank Like A Boss* provides clear and easy-to-digest guidelines coupled with helpful anecdotes and tangible suggestions that apply to the success of all businesses as they mature. If you're trying to maximize the benefit of your banking relationship, don't miss this book. If you're a banker, this book would make a great gift for your business clients!"

Lori Bettinger, Co-President
Alliance Partners

Richard Barbercheck's business acumen and expert approach to the relationship between businesses and banks jumps off the page in *Bank Like A Boss*. The balance between the two is so well articulated that you can immediately implement the prescribed best practices. Richard has distilled down a career of expertise for the reader's benefit. I will personally revisit this often, as the charted path is a prescription for success.

Noah Berkheimer, Chief Support Officer
Beneficial Talent Source

Every small business owner can benefit from reading *Bank Like A Boss*! The author, a former bank executive with decades of experience, takes you behind the curtain of the banking industry. He explains in plain English what you need to know to be the kind of business that banks love to say YES to, despite the economy!

Christine Luken,
Founder of the Financial Dignity® Movement & author of
Money is Emotional: Prevent Your Heart from Hijacking Your Wallet

BANK LIKE A BOSS

How Entrepreneurs Maintain Access to Cash in Good Times and Bad

CONTENTS

CHAPTER 1
WHY BANKABILITY AFFECTS ACCESS TO CASH

In order for a business to maintain access to cash in good times and bad they need to be bankable. By definition, bankability is nothing more than the ability of a business or individual to qualify as a bank's borrower. Due to the requirements associated with qualification, being bankable becomes somewhat of a barometer for health of a business. This doesn't hold true in every instance because the requirements to borrow differ between banks. But, in general, all of them are assessing the potential risk to solid future financial performance of the borrowing business. The less risk, the higher the likelihood of solid financial performance and the more bankable the business.

From this perspective, if a business focuses on maintaining a strong bankable position, they will likely have access to cash in good times and bad. A strong financial condition in business is one of the most critical factors of being bankable. One way to evaluate the financial condition of a business is to look at their cash position, profitability, and leverage. An easy way to remember this is "Cash is King." Your Income Statement, representing profitability, is "Queen," and your Balance Sheet, representing leverage, is your "Castle Fortress." Cash allows the business to operate and expand. Profitability allows the business to retain cash as a reserve that can be accessed during challenging times. Cash is accumulated as an asset and it builds the strength of the balance sheet allowing even greater protection from adverse circumstances.

Banks are a primary source of cash and maintaining access to it by being bankable provides a much greater chance for success. The purpose of this book is to provide critical insight on how to position your business as bankable, in good times and bad.

AN INTRODUCTION TO THE VALUE OF BANKABILITY

I never really did what I intended. Although I didn't grow up on a farm, I did grow up in the "Breadbasket of the World," Champaign County, Illinois. Illinois is one of the Midwest states known for some of the highest grain production yields in the world, and Champaign County was one of the top producing counties. When I was in high school, I became interested in agriculture and followed my interest into college, obtaining my Bachelor of Science degree in Agribusiness Economics from Southern Illinois University. I fully intended to pursue a career in the support of agricultural production and secured my first job selling A. O. Smith Harvestore feed systems to livestock producers.

As luck would have it, 1980 was the beginning of the greatest recession in agriculture since the Great Depression. Throughout the decade of the 1970's, agriculture production enjoyed a phenomenal expansion due to the development of higher yielding crops, improved mechanical and machinery production systems, and improved production techniques. For virtually the first time in history we were able to produce food at a rate that could feed the world. But we didn't.

The advanced production and resulting inventories of grain soon outpaced the world's ability to purchase. In other words, the expansion of our production ability vastly surpassed the expansion of the world economies that would pay for the food. Additionally, throughout the expansion period producers were encouraged by government and education to borrow money to adopt these new methods and expand production operations. This created huge leverage positions on producer balance sheets that went well beyond reasonable risk management, coupled with the fact that for generations much leverage of any kind was avoided in this industry. Therefore, we had an extremely high risk financial situation with an industry that had no experience on how to manage it. As that situation consumed the industry, commodity prices fell, due to oversupply and the inability to market the surplus, to an unprofitable level causing a dramatic level of default on the debt that had been incurred. This was quickly followed by a record number of farm failures and foreclosures.

It was near the beginning of this crisis that I began selling feed systems to farmers that didn't have any money nor capacity to borrow. I soon found myself sitting at farm kitchen tables working with producers, trying to find a way for them to improve their financial situation and survive. Needless to say, it was very self-serving. If I could get their finances structured properly, maybe they could afford the quarter of a million dollar feed systems I was selling. Sometimes it worked, most times it didn't. But I loved my job. I was outdoors working to help the hardest working, salt-of-the-earth people I'd ever met. I controlled my own schedule and built phenomenal relationships. But I wasn't making much money.

One day I was in a bank presenting a producer's business plan that justified their investment in purchasing the equipment I was selling. I needed the bank to finance it. Following my presentation, the banker asked if I'd be interested in working for the bank. I promptly responded that there was no way I would give up my comfortable life to work in an office.

Let's just say a few hungry months later I changed my mind and became the bank's first Agricultural Lending Specialist. My job was to "stop the bleeding." To work with their borrowers to find acceptable survival strategies that would get the bank repaid. The beginning of my banking career. And while I didn't realize it at the time, the beginning of my coaching career.

In those early years, I spent about a third of my time in the Federal Bankruptcy Court working through restructure and liquidation plans. I found myself on the front end of repossession activities on farms as well as businesses. Another third of my time was working with borrowers to fulfill their financial plans and find creditworthy borrowers to replace those that failed. And the final third of my time was providing education, literally classroom education, on financial management to agricultural producers and businesses.

As my career moved on, I spent the next 35 years working with businesses in virtually any industry (banking included) to survive recessions, economic slowdowns, and negative circumstantial situations. It is only appropriate that I essentially finalized my banking career in the fall of 2016 as the Corporate Chief Credit Officer of the then $8.5 billion First Financial Bank based in Cincinnati, Ohio, having worked with the bank and its borrowers to survive and thrive through the Great Recession of 2007.

This book is intended to provide business owners and executives, as well as bankers, a perspective on how to position for tough times. It is my hope that you take away some tangible activities that will definitely improve your access to cash during future growth opportunities or challenges in your business and tips for managing your banking relationship. For the bankers, this should provide you a perspective on the real meaning of relationship management and, when deployed appropriately, provide for a portfolio of strong performing businesses, in good times and bad.

During my 35 years in the commercial banking industry, I worked with businesses through five definitive recessions and several economic slowdowns. The deep recessions of the early 1980's and 2007 provided unique and in-depth perspectives on how dangerously devastating tough economic times can be for any business. At the same time, it was apparent that some businesses thrived despite the challenges. This impact on businesses was evidenced in varying degrees during all the recessions, economic slowdowns, and negative circumstantial situations that occurred over those 35 years.

From a banking perspective, during these challenging times it became apparent that some businesses suffered more than others. In fact, some businesses, even if they weren't counter-cyclical, seemed to benefit during tough times. At the same time, other businesses were burning through cash trying to regain their financial performance or, worse yet, trying to survive, looking for bank loans to help bridge the cash flow gap. Others were financially stable but looking for cash to fund increased operating costs due to businesses expansion created by new customer acquisition or to capitalize on the opportunity to acquire competitors or complimentary businesses at discount prices.

In various positions of lending, administration, analysis, review, and adjudicating credit in bank portfolios it was my task to identify the differences between these businesses and to predict the potential risk of loss in the credit portfolio. In essence, I had to determine, "What's the difference?" This triggered a desire to observe what happens to businesses and banks during tough economic times and what differentiates the winners from the losers in this all-important game of business performance and survival.

It's important to recognize that while, at first, it looks like these impacts only affected the borrowers, the reality was that it was having an impact on non-borrowing businesses as well. Even less evident was the fact that banks were experiencing many of the same challenges and being impacted with similar results.

Therefore, the investigation began. What characteristics were evident in each of these environments that could point to cause and effect? Were these characteristics similar in each situation or did each business, industry, or event have its unique challenges? Was this just a result of chance or destiny, or was something else going on? If we could figure out the unique characteristics of businesses that thrived in tough times, regardless of industry, could we promote those characteristics to all businesses? If we could, it would provide for a foundation upon which they could improve or sustain performance, even in tough times.

When the ability to borrow is limited, or eliminated, the life blood of the organization is impaired. It must now survive on operating cash flows and/or the injection of cash from owners or investors. This generates a significant financial and emotional stress that distracts the management from focusing on business improvement strategies, operational course corrections, or crisis management. This is why I set out to answer the question: how can businesses prepare in a manner that would ensure survival through access to cash, their continued successful performance, or growth?

As you read further you may find ideas and concepts that appear difficult to accept or implement. Please recognize that each business applies these concepts in a manner that provides the appropriate benefit to its own organization. The reader must also recognize that history has evidenced these concepts to be essentially effective and, if implemented, to have a definitive difference in the experience businesses have in tough economic times.

In using this information each business should plan, execute, and evaluate in an ongoing repetitive process to fully capitalize on the benefits of this information. As bankers read this book, they should recognize that they play a significant role in shaping the future of the businesses within their portfolios. Providing businesses with insight and education on these principals is a value-added proposition that banking has relinquished over several decades of focus on sales rather than relationship. Working with businesses to ensure their bankability over time is a win-win for all involved.

Here's wishing all readers and their respective businesses the best of success, in good times and bad. Enjoy the journey!

CHAPTER 2
HOW BANKING WORKS
& WHY IT MATTERS

In order for a business to be bankable, management needs to understand how banking works. This provides insight into why banks have certain borrowing requirements and conditions, expect certain loan structures, and don't always say yes. Because most businesses rely upon bank loans for their access to cash, we need to understand how banks work.

The fundamentals of a bank's operating model impact how and why banks make the decisions they do and impose the processes they use. When people think of banks, they often think of large impressive looking vaults full of money. Banks and bankers are even portrayed in movies and the media as the stingy old bankers that have and control all the money. Due to this perspective and portrayal, understanding what banks do, and why, becomes distorted.

At the most basic level, neither bankers nor banks own the money in the vault, the public does! It's critical that we understand this, because it is the underlying component of the banking industry that governs their behaviors and your access to that money.

When you, your mother, your grandfather, your children, neighbor, colleague, co-worker, your friend, or anyone else for that matter, deposits money into the bank, they do so with the expectation that they can get that money back whenever they demand it. That's why checking accounts are called "Demand Accounts." Everyone working in the bank, from the CEO to the entry level clerk, is charged with and responsible for ensuring the safety of those funds.

For banks to make money, they use those deposits to make loans. Therefore, the public's money is not in the bank. It's in the hands of the borrowers. If that money doesn't eventually make its way back to the bank as planned, they may not have the money to provide to the depositors when they demand it. If this seems like a stretch, just think about the characteristics of the Great Depression in the 1930's or bank failures you've heard about in the past. In many cases, that's essentially what happened. The payments being made on loans (or not being made in this case) and the other sources of cash were not adequate to ensure that the public could get its money back. That's when banks fail and regulators step in to protect the public's deposits.

Just like any other business, banks need to be profitable. To do this, they generally charge more for the loans than they pay for the deposits. The technical term for this is called "arbitrage," borrowing money (gathering deposits) at one rate, and loaning it to others at a higher rate, thereby profiting on the difference between the two. Why do banks need to make a profit? The same reason you do - to generate a return to the owners, the investors or shareholders that own the business. And, without a gross profit you can't pay your operating cost, and soon you're out of business. Would you rather they use your deposited money to pay the operating costs?

So, banks borrow money from the public and loan it out to those that need cash. You're probably asking, if not screaming, "So why can't I get access to the cash when I need it?" Well, it's all about risk and protecting the deposits of the public and the earnings of the bank that keep it in business. As we begin to discuss bankability, and a business's access to cash, keep this risk/reward concept in mind. It drives everything

CHAPTER 3
WHAT ARE THE CHANCES
OF BUSINESS SUCCESS?

The cause for business failure typically occurs in the Market, Team, and/or Capital positions. Name any reason for a known business failure and I'll bet it will fit into one of these three categories. Small and Medium Business (SMB) failure occurs more frequently than you might realize. This book focuses predominately on the capital and/or cash component, but you may find references to market or team impacts as well.

The US Bureau of Labor Statistics indicates that roughly 20% of all SMB's fail within their first year, 33% within their second, 50% within 5 years, and 66% within 10 years. Wow! SMB's have a whopping 33% of surviving beyond 10 years. If your business has survived beyond 10 years, congratulations! Great job. You've made it through the toughest times and have a great foundation for future success. If your business is less than 10 years old and those numbers didn't get you to throw the book against the wall and give up, keep reading.

As I referenced previously, "Cash is King." I could write a book on this phrase alone but suffice it to say that when you have access to cash you have the ability to buy time to solve the Market and Team issues that may arise. Without it, you don't stand a chance. Therein lies the reason this book is focused on access to cash. Your cash sources are definable as your reserves, your cash flow, and access to third party cash (investors and loans). That's it.

So, if you want to increase your chances of survival or success, ALWAYS manage your access to cash!

CHAPTER 4
THE BUSINESS LIFE CYCLE'S IMPACT ON ACCESS TO CASH

In every phase of the business life cycle the definition of bankability changes. You need to know where your business is in the cycle to better understand what you need to do to establish and maintain bankability.

Given that most businesses don't survive for more than five years, you would think that a chapter on the business life cycle to be relatively short. But many businesses do survive beyond the initial five years and yet they are still at risk of failure at any point during the business life cycle. Therefore, it's important for us to take a look at the business life cycle as it affects all businesses regardless of how long they've been in operation.

The business life cycle includes four phases, some of which should repeat over time, IF the business is good enough to maneuver through the fourth phase effectively. As a precursor to Bank-Ability, one needs to understand where they are in the business life cycle. We'll examine each phase and look at some of the challenges that occur, thereby driving the need for a bankability strategy throughout each phase. Given the different characteristics that exist in each phase, the strategies will differ; focused priorities and expectations for financial performance will change. So, we start with the Business Life Cycle.

The first three Phases in the Business Life Cycle include the Learning Phase, Growth Phase, and the Decline or Mature Phase. These phases are represented in the graphic below known as The Sigmoid Curve. The Sigmoid Curve is essentially an algebraic formula known as the Sigmoid function. The formula shows that every growth curve will experience different rates of growth over time and eventually flatten, and then decline, unless it is interrupted. While the Sigmoid Curve clearly indicates the Growth Phase in a business life cycle, the fundamental point of the curve is that nothing grows forever without change to the current state of operations. The current state of business operations is defined in the assumptions that we use to make significant decisions that drive the business forward.

But why would we change the current state of operations if we're in the Growth Phase? Isn't it logical to approach the Growth Phase with the philosophy that "if it isn't broke, don't fix it?" It would seem so, but if we do, and ignore our responsibility to anticipate change, we risk having performance drop off before we react. Ideally, we anticipate change and adjust our operations in a way that allows us to reinvest resources such that they sustain and extend the Growth Phase.

Therefore, the Growth Phase is interrupted near its peak by the Reinvestment Phase. If it isn't, when a business reaches the Mature or Decline or Mature Phase, it is faced with a critical decision. Depending upon the decisions made at this juncture the business may decline and eventually die, or it may, through appropriate reinvestment of resources, reposition to an earlier phase that extends and accentuates its life. But let's start at the beginning, the Learning Phase.

SIGMOID CURVE – BUSINESS LIFE CYCLE

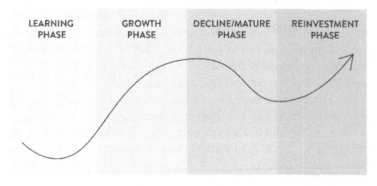

| LEARNING PHASE | GROWTH PHASE | DECLINE/MATURE PHASE | REINVESTMENT PHASE |

LIFE CYCLE CHARACTERISITICS

LEARNING PHASE

In the Learning Phase, a business is in the early Phases of its existence and undergoing all the difficulties associated with the unknown. It is exploratory in nature, and even if it's in a well-known industry with a well-developed plan, the business in question typically hasn't experienced or proven how to effectively execute. In other words, there's just a lot of experimenting and "on-the-job training." As the business begins to experience results, the business owner(s) or manager(s) must implement a multitude of appropriate course corrections needed to succeed.

This leads to a period of exciting chaos. The business is extraordinarily busy with numerous challenges and difficulties that are distracting from the expected smooth operation. It seems like every time you have it "figured out" something else changes to challenge that smooth operation. You know, it's like a "Whack-A-Mole" game where when you push one button down another one pops up.

This perpetual trying of new things and learning from mistakes creates a difficult environment for achieving intended results. It becomes a literal scramble to get the results you're looking for. It's frustrating, stressful, nerve wracking, and downright tiring. You're thinking, "I got into this business to be my own boss, manage my destiny, have a better work-life balance, and make the money I want rather than rely upon a paycheck, and all I'm doing is chasing my tail."

Do you know why most businesses don't survive during their first five years? Many just run out of will power. They exhaust their fortitude to keep moving forward. There have been too many roadblocks, too many trips, and too many falls. They just reach the end of the rope and let go. The other reason most businesses don't survive beyond five years is money. They run out of money. The cost of getting the business to a sustainable profitability exceeds their capacity or willingness to continue subsidizing the operation.

Many businesses in the Learning Phase aren't bankable due to the multitude of unknowns that are characteristic of early stage businesses. Therefore, many of them start by self-funding the operations through personal savings, or they have a significant customer providing enough cash flow to keep the bills paid as they attempt to grow. To achieve bankability in the Learning Phase is difficult. If a business wants bank financing at this point, it is critical that they have very detailed plans regarding their market, their team, and their operations. These plans need to reasonably evidence that a broad range of outcomes can support loan repayment. Even then, a bank may require enhancements to the loan, such as a Small Business Administration (SBA) guarantee.

There are a few secrets to surviving the Learning Phase. First, stay focused. When you embarked on this adventure, you had a vision. You might not have had much of a plan, but you had a vision. That vision may not be written down in a vision statement hanging on your wall, but you had one all the same. You knew what you wanted out of this. Focus on that. If all your challenges are course corrected with that vision in mind, you will eventually reach your goal. But you have to chart those course corrections based on that vision, every time. If you lose sight of the vision, if it isn't the driving force behind your decisions, you'll stray. Eventually you'll stray too far and there may be no coming back. Remember, you're in the Learning Phase and if you stray too far from the intended outcome it may take you to a point where you don't know how, or don't have the resources, to find your way back.

In the Learning Phase, when I say, "stay focused," I mean you should apply a "hard focus" on your target(s). Let me explain. I enjoy the sport of shooting sporting clays. In sporting clays, the shooter fires a shotgun to break a moving orange target about the size of a drink coaster. These targets are thrown from a machine at various speeds and angles to the shooter. Tracking the movement of these targets can be challenging at best. As I worked with my coach, he would admonish me when he recognized that I was applying a casual focus to the target. When I did this, it didn't mean that I didn't see the target, or that I wasn't tracking it or making course corrections, I was. But with a casual focus I'd inevitably miss the target. In sporting clays, a miss is a miss, and a break is a break, no "almost" points given. When this happened, my coach would encourage me to apply a "hard focus" on the target. Don't see anything else, don't react to anything else; all you should see and react to is the target and its movement. When I did that, I broke the target.

The same applies to your focus when you're in the Learning Phase. There's a ton of distraction. Stay focused. Apply a hard focus on your target(s) and you'll achieve your objectives. Eventually, your ability to focus on your targets will become somewhat second nature. It will be more comfortable as you correct missteps and reapply successful strategies and tactics.

The second way to ensure your business survives through the Learning Phase is to simply not give up. I know it sounds trite, but it's true. I had a boss once that believed he'd win on every business deal he ever made. His philosophy was "I'll never be beat if I just keep getting up every time they knock me down." As simple as that sounds, it's extremely difficult, but it's right. Perseverance wins the day in most endeavors.

Finally, but not the least of these, you must implement a "Plan, Execute, Evaluate, Repeat" strategy from the start, and at every major decision you make. Build this discipline as a habit and it'll serve you at every turn, no matter what phase you're in. You have the option to plan and execute, decide if it worked, and if it didn't, take another direction. But if you do that, you'll have wasted valuable time and resources. If you take the time to evaluate what happened, to look critically at the effort in context with the objective, you'll likely find that you were moving in the right direction and only slightly off course. If you make a course correction rather than go back and start over, you have a strong probability that you'll get where you wanted to be more efficiently and effectively. If you give up on it, it's a "start over," a "Go back to GO and do not collect $200." Typically, not a good result.

As I started my business, Strategic Orientation, LLC, I began to feel that course correction was the business objective. Every time I felt like I had things figured out, something would muck up the works and I was back to the drawing board. Here's an example. When I decided that business coaching was the right space for me, I researched 8 to 10 companies that provided business content and support for coaching activity. I didn't want to have to create all my own content when others had already developed valuable tools for business owners to use. I found a franchise that essentially licensed their content and allowed me a lot of discretion regarding client selection and the application of the content. It also didn't restrict me with a territory. This was great, I was the only franchisee in my state. Therefore, I invested in branding my company with the franchisor name. I was set. I was out there networking and selling, getting the market to recognize me and my company as the perfect blend of business expertise and proven content. Then without notice the franchisor put three other franchisees smack dab in the middle of my ideal client market.

Guess what? They all wanted to brand their companies with the franchisor name. While we all offered similar content, we all operated in independent businesses essentially competing for the same clients. Sound confusing? It was, and there didn't seem to be a good answer from the franchisor or the franchisee group. Therefore, I found myself needing to rebrand my company in order to retain the momentum I had in branding myself as the "go to" business coaching provider in the market. Talk about a course correction. It was expensive, time consuming, and definitely frustrating. Well, I relearned what I already knew. I was in the Learning Phase.

Once you've evaluated the situation, identified the necessary course corrections, implement the changes, and repeat it. That's what learning is all about.

GROWTH PHASE

The Growth Phase of the business life cycle is the most enthusiastic and energizing phase. This phase is filled with high energy and exhilaration. Everyone in the business feels the momentum as the business is growing and sales are accelerating. It's when business owners begin to realize that they seem to have things figured out and results are occurring at or better than the levels they expected. This enthusiastic environment generates new possibilities and ideas that seem to be coming from everywhere on how to accentuate the success. You've probably heard the saying, "Success Breeds Success." Well, there's some truth in this. That next success is found through the energy built off the previous success. It's a little bit like one of Newton's Laws, essentially, "An object in motion tends to stay in motion...." Activity, ideas, processes, and resources used in previous success strategies are leveraged to find and achieve new success strategies. It's a great time in the business life cycle, and great companies tend to capitalize on this to achieve phenomenal results.

As company growth continues, the needs of the company begin to outpace the contributions of the owners, managers, and staff. Some of the skill sets, knowledge, and resources originally brought by the owners to begin the business and bring it to this point reach a limitation. In order for them to continue a positive growth path, they must realize when these limitations begin to appear and plan accordingly. At this point it will be important for them to delegate certain tasks and decision making. They may even need to bring in additional management or production talent to enhance the skills, knowledge, and resources of the company.

Management needs to be looking forward, envisioning what the company will look like in the near and distant future. They need to consider the challenges to that vision, and in doing so they will increase the chance of seeing potential problems before they materialize. I call this "Forward Looking Risk Appropriate Management." Welcome to business in the Growth Phase. It's messy, but this is where the best sausage is really made.

The challenges encountered by the organization aren't just related to internal operations. A company doesn't spontaneously grow; it grows over time, and it doesn't grow in a straight line either. It encounters starts and stops, hurdles and roadblocks on its initiatives, sales efforts, and operations. And all the while your company is growing things are changing outside the company as well. These external impacts can catch us by surprise. Things like a changing economy, new laws and regulations, someone invents a "better mousetrap," new competition, pandemics, and a myriad of other events challenge our Growth Phase.

Some companies seem to manage all these challenges with ease, course correcting and pivoting as the need arises. Done appropriately and timely, it will extend the Growth Phase, and they will enjoy a continuation of their success. That's the good news.

The bad news is that "The worst enemy of success is success." As companies and individuals experience success they tend to become complacent. They've worked hard to get to this point and there's a sub-conscious, if not conscious, perspective that they can take a breather, calm down and enjoy the fruits of success. But this very perspective is one of the things that keeps them from seeing what's really happening. No matter how much we want to avoid it, things change. Things change every day, every moment of every day. This seems obvious, but we don't like to admit it, and we certainly fatigue from dealing with it. Therefore, we enjoy the perceived benefit that success brings, and we feel like we can relax and just let the success continue.

Well, I'm sorry to be the bearer of bad news, but that dog won't hunt. It just isn't realistic. Change impacts everything we do. Let's say that success was predicated on acquiring key customers, or developing highly efficient processes; all it takes is one customer to change their needs, or a supplier to change their process, and suddenly you find yourself in a scramble trying to regain your footing. The very thing that made you successful is now your greatest challenge.

A colleague of mine worked for a community bank during its Growth Phase. When she started with the organization, they were about $2.5 billion in size. Over the course of her 8 years with this organization they grew in size by $7 billion dollars. That's over $500 million per year! Can you imagine the rate of change? Everything from product to market, from processes to facilities and staffing would be in a perpetual state of evaluation, creation, and redevelopment.

The organization was managed with focused individuals that orchestrated these changes with enthusiasm. Nobody was afraid to course correct, it was a daily event. The organization had a very energized, enthusiastic, forward looking approach built upon a culture of teamwork and mutual respect. Unfortunately, due to economic and internal circumstances the rate of growth slowed, and management found themselves uncomfortable. They would implement course correction strategies, but weren't comfortable with the time and processes necessary for them to deliver results. They were too accustomed with a fast paced changing environment. So, what did they do? They changed.

Every 6 to 9 months a new strategy, structure, or approach would be rolled out. This is what they were used to. They didn't recognize that the very frequency of changes slowed the time to results. Management and staff became frustrated, seeing what appeared to be change for change sake. Frustrated, many of them left. Executive management decided to rearrange the organizational structure placing other, less qualified individuals into new positions of responsibility, only exacerbating the problem. The growth continued to slow, talent continued to leave, and eventually the organization merged and adopted the operating model of the acquired organization. A great organization had gone by the wayside because success became its greatest enemy.

The key is flexibility. If management stays vigilant and proactively addresses challenges and opportunities, they will minimize the negative impacts of change. If they embrace and effectively initiate change for the betterment of the company, they will enjoy an elongated Growth Phase. But in order to do this they need a strong visionary component in their thought process.

In the Growth Phase, businesses have the opportunity to increase their bankability through proven results. The more successful the company is at achieving consistent positive financial returns the more they increase their bankability. They are essentially decreasing the uncertainty, or the risk, that was characteristic of the Learning Phase. However, a business can survive in the Growth Phase and yet struggle to achieve consistent positive returns. When this happens, they will struggle with bankability as well. I'll come back to this later, but a secret to increasing bankability in the Growth Phase is managing the retained earnings.

DECLINE OR MATURE PHASE

This Decline or Mature Phase follows a prolonged period of meeting or exceeding expectations. All the excitement and enthusiasm enjoyed during the Growth Phase begins to diminish. The company may begin to experience fewer sales, less exciting results, and reap fewer rewards for their efforts causing profit and/or margins to shrink. With these challenges, morale declines and people become frustrated and less enamored with the work environment. Why? Everything was going so well.

In the Decline or Mature Phase, the business and personal habits of owners and managers become less effective. The business processes, marketing, delivery, and management practices aren't as efficient or competitive. Why not? Because things change. Not just internal business things, but everything around us changes. As we become accustomed to our regular routines, the world moves on regardless.

As you may imagine, if businesses are less than effective in the Growth Phase the business will begin to decline. Additionally, if the industry changes through new market demands, transformation, or disrupters, the business may find itself in the Decline or Mature Phase.

Maybe it's best to provide a couple of examples here. First, let's look at the Decline or Mature Phase. Consider the auto industry. Since its invention, the automobile has been continuously manufactured. But, over time the automobile companies found themselves struggling to survive. Changes that occurred started to outpace their ability to adjust. Production processes and materials, human resource management and labor practices, consumer wants, and expectations all changed. There was still a market for automobiles, but many companies in the industry found themselves in the Decline or Mature Phase.

Consider a company like IBM. In the 1980's and 90's IBM was at the forefront of computing technology. As the industry progressed at a rapid rate, it became difficult to compete due to rapid change requirements. It was quicker and more efficient for new companies to enter the market, time and time again, with new and updated technology. Over thirty to forty years, IBM found itself in and out of the Decline or Mature Phase several times. Today, it is quite a different company than when it started, but it is still very successful.

Let's contrast that to a mature company. The age-old example is the manufacturer of buggy whips. For years, horses provided the primary mode of transportation and horse and/or buggy whips were in high and regular demand. As the market moved to other modes of transportation, - bicycles, trains, autos, etc. - fewer and fewer buggy whips were needed. This industry had essentially run its course. Certainly, a company that made buggy whips could evolve into something else and survive, but essentially the buggy whip industry was gone. It had matured and virtually died.

Here's one that has predominately evolved over the course of most of our lives. Think about the delivery of music, or for that matter, sound in general. A century ago, music was presented almost entirely in person through live presentation. If you were in the business of providing live entertainment, your world was about to change dramatically.

The Victrola Phonograph came on the scene in 1925. By 1948, it was being replaced with Long Play Vinyl Records. The Tape Recorder was invented in 1935 and provided the base for the Compact Cassette Tapes in 1963, soon to be followed by 8 Track Tapes Cartridges in 1965. Then in 1982 Compact Discs (CD's) were introduced followed by the introduction of the Internet (World Wide Web) in 1989. Soon to follow were MP3 Players (1995), the iPod (2001), and now much of our music is listened to through the Internet Cloud where we can store our own library of music.

Navigating this pace of change through the maturation of the industry required a lot of foresight and re-investment. Bankability can be maintained throughout the Decline or Mature Phase as long as the organization maintains good financial performance and reserves. However, as financial performance wanes and reserves are depleted, the financial trends and position of the company will deteriorate, increasing the risk and decreasing their bankability. Eventually, poor performance will eliminate their bankability and other sources of capital and/or cash may be required.

Any company in the Decline or Mature Phase has a choice, they can either ride the industry curve doing what they're doing and eventually die off, or they can reinvest and give the company new life. This brings us to the Reinvestment Phase.

REINVESTMENT PHASE

All three of the previous business life cycle phases are pretty much a given. They happen, like it or not. The Reinvestment Phase is optional. If an organization is going to survive, a return to essential Strategic Planning is critical. This reinvestment initiative is multi-faceted and can't just be an additional cash injection. As a matter of fact, many companies in the Decline or Mature Phase are flush with cash they've accumulated during the Growth Phase.

Because more is at stake, the Strategic Planning for re-investment must look at all aspects of the company. Everything from their core market and products, to production, marketing, and internal management must be considered. Just as important is reconsidering the Vision and Mission of the organization. It may have changed and a deep understanding of what those look like going forward is necessary. The Strategic Planning process shown in the following image includes a Business Plan component that is often overlooked during the Strategic Planning process. But it shouldn't be.

In addition to the Vision, Mission, and Values, a strong Strategic Plan includes Objectives, Goals, Strategies, and Measures. This approach to a Strategic Plan is only valuable to the growth of the organization if those components are supported with a strong Business Plan. Depending on the degree of change, this may be as comprehensive as that used for a startup business. In the Reinvestment Phase, the Business Plan components outlined should be given significant consideration. The degree to which any of them are addressed will depend upon the degree of change anticipated for the organization, but all of them should be considered. These are the factors that will allow your company to continue its success.

STRATEGIC PLANNING PROCESS
DURING REINVESTMENT PHASE

VALUES   OBJECTIVES

VISION   GOALS

MISSION   STRATEGIES

MEASURES

BUSINESS PLAN

1. The Company
   a. Definition of the needs the company will satisfy
   b. Products and Services offered to satisfy those needs
2. Market Analysis
   a. Target Market Characteristics (Demographic, Geographic, Psychographic, etc.)
   b. Target Market Size
   c. Ideal Client/Customer Definition
3. Product/Service Development Requirements
   a. Project Management Plan
   b. Major Milestone Deadlines
4. Marketing & Sales Plan
   a. Marketing Strategy
   b. Sales Strategy & Process
   c. Keys to Competitive Success
5. Organizational & Personnel
   a. Key Personnel (Ownership, Management, Operational, etc.)
   b. Operational & Production Model
6. Financial Plan
   a. Capital Requirements

   b. Operational Budget & Monitoring Plan
   c. Financial Forecasting Plan
   d. Cash Flow Projections
   e. Financing Requirements

Completing the Strategic and Business Plans for reinvestment may indicate that there will be a significant demand on cash, and while the company may have accumulated some from the Growth Phase, it may not be adequate to finance the necessary changes identified in the Strategic Planning process for reinvestment. With this information company owners, shareholders, and managers are able to make a conscious decision about the future direction of the company.

This happened to a company I was working with that had been in existence for 75 years. It was family owned and under third generation leadership. The current leadership was about to experience a senior management change due to a long term leader's retirement, and the company was taking a fresh look at where they were. They were in the Decline or Mature Phase. They realized they needed to do something soon and set out three major objectives.

Their first objective was to bring the company into the 20th century. In their due diligence, they found that their products, services, technology, and processes had fallen significantly behind the industry. Second, they needed to drastically regain market share. The organization was suffering from a huge negative reputation coupled with newer, fierce competition. And it was taking a measurable toll. Third, while they had amassed a war chest of funds over the years, they recognized that to accomplish all that was needed, it would challenge their capital position. In summary, their objectives were as follows:

1. Move into the 20th century.
2. Regain lost market share.
3. Commit to funding the change through earnings, capital, and contributions if necessary.

Correcting all of this took 5 years, and they were lucky enough to have preserved profitability, barely at times, and come through the re-investment with an adequate capital position to continue their newfound growth. Obviously, there's a lot more to that story, but that's meant for another book. The point is, the Reinvestment Phase can be very costly and time consuming. The sooner it's recognized the better.

LIFE CYCLE TRAPS AND WHAT TO AVOID

Throughout all these life cycle phases there are traps. If owners fall into these traps, the business is likely to stall, if not fail, and may not make it into the next phase. As business owners navigate these phases it's critical that they avoid these traps in order to maintain bankability. So, let's take some time to identify and describe the typical (but not all) the traps that are encountered.

SIGMOID CURVE – BUSINESS LIFE CYCLE

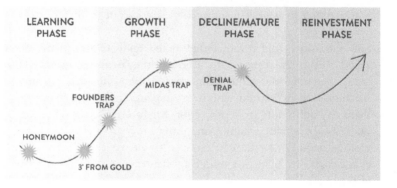

HONEYMOON TRAP

In the Learning Phase, the first trap is oftentimes referred to as the "Honeymoon Trap." This trap, as the name infers, happens very soon after the establishment or major re-invention of the business. Everyone involved in this new direction and venture is excited and enthusiastic about the future and, as typical in a new marriage, no one is thinking of the challenges ahead. Why should they? They've been preparing and dreaming about this day for some time. Now it's here, everything's great! Isn't it? Well, it is. It really is great. The only problem is that the enthusiasm distracts us from the things we need to be doing or thinking about. Remember, my story about shooting sporting clays and the need to apply a "Hard Focus" on the target; and, that if we had a casual focus on the target are chances of success were negatively impacted? Well, that's what's happening in the Honeymoon Trap.

Business owners that fall into the "Honeymoon Trap" have sometimes mistaken the very aspect of starting the business as the goal. Well, they've achieved it. Now what? To avoid this trap, use a hard focus on longer-term objectives and a well devised plan. In doing so, you'll be rewarded with better results and greater success.

THREE FEET FROM GOLD

If the business avoids the Honeymoon Trap, they'll continue working hard to get to operational and financial stability. This is hard work. It really is! It's easy to get tired, fatigued, confused, and frustrated when you're trying to establish a new business or strategic direction.

Someone once told me that they hated budgets and plans. When I asked why, they responded, "Because they're never right." This in many ways is the underlying reason new business owners get frustrated. They started with a great plan, so why isn't it working? Plans, by definition are a projection for future events. They are built on past experiences, assumptions about a myriad of circumstances, and various degrees of educated guesses about what might happen. The chances of any plans, or budgets, occurring exactly as designed are virtually non-existent.

I find marketing plans to be the most frustrating because they seem to be fraught with a much higher degree of uncertainty. And these are the most critical for a new business. If the marketing plan isn't successful, there will not be enough sales; not enough sales, no business.

In any event the frustration continues to mount. There's so much to do other than produce a widget or provide a service. Now you're handling shipping, receiving, inventory, marketing, HR, facilities, legal and accounting, and now they want you to handle sales!?! Sound familiar? Even if a company provides adequate capital to move through the Learning Phase, these frustrations, and the stress that comes with them cause many business owners to just give up. Probably when they're "Three Feet from Gold."

The name of this trap comes from the story of a gold miner that dug and chipped, and hammered away at the rock in his mine shaft to the point of frustration. He finally gave up and sold the mine for a discounted price to another miner. The new miner removed three feet of rock and found the gold. Don't quit too soon, give it everything you've got.

FOUNDER'S TRAP

We find the "Founder's Trap" in the early stages of the Growth Phase of the Business Life Cycle. At the time the Founder's Trap shows up, things are going well. The business has made it out of the Learning Phase and is beginning to gain momentum. As the business grows, it increasingly puts a burden on the owner ("founder") to keep up. They have managed to successfully perform under the many hats necessary to get this business up and running. But as the business continues to grow, their ability to successfully manage the ever-increasing demands limit the company growth. The owner believes that they are solely responsible for the success of the business, that it requires them to be involved in all aspects of the business, and that no one else is adequately skilled to handle these decisions.

If the owner stays in this mindset, they're likely to stymy the company's progress, frustrate key employees, and/or fall short of accomplishing business objectives to the point of settling for current performance with limited, if any growth, selling the business to new leadership or closing it, out of frustration and/or lack of performance.

No one builds long term successful companies by themselves. Recognize the need to grow employees, hire those that can bring added value to the organization, and orchestrate the activities as a leader that allows the company to continue its growth and success. Your role is changing from an Owner/Manager to an Owner/Leader. Embrace it or risk falling into this trap.

MIDAS TRAP

Further along in the Growth Phase lies the "Midas Trap." The "Midas Trap" shows up when the company has enjoyed a long run of success and is well into the Growth Phase of the business life cycle. You have managed to overcome the initial exuberance of starting a business, pushed through the challenges of the Learning Phase, and learned how to lead the organization through continued growth. Therefore, you think, "We've got this." That's exactly when the Midas Trap shows up. The legend of King Midas is popularly remembered in Greek mythology for his ability to turn everything he touched into gold. The trap shows up at a time when ownership and management have a sense of confidence that they've got it figured out. And they must, right? I mean it's working and working well.

The very complacency that comes along with this success and confidence is the Achilles' heel to the continued success of the company. Over-confident leadership can become blinded to the ever-changing environment and the need for continuous improvement. Without recognition of these outside forces, they begin to negatively impact the company.

To overcome this trap, management needs to be constantly challenging the status quo. That means the business is likely to experience a degree of constant change. We've all heard that we must "embrace change" in the work environment. And I believe that generally to be true, but I caution managers that perpetually look for opportunities to change just because it's different or because they can put their stamp of accomplishment on the change effort. Change for change sake can cause significant damage to an organization's morale and momentum.

Make sure that the continuous improvement process includes a good deal of due diligence and vetting before implementing change. Just because something isn't working exactly like you intended doesn't necessarily indicate that the effort was all wrong, sometimes it just needs an adjustment to be successful. Management's job here is to be vigilant, yet prudent, when identifying a need to change and implementing new directions.

DENIAL TRAP

As we continue to move along the Growth Phase of the curve, we can reach a point near the Decline or Mature Phase where things are going ok, but our momentum may have slowed, and the market seems to be ambivalent to our products or services. In other words, while we're still viable we appear a little lackluster. Performance and momentum just aren't what they used to be. We may even be experiencing a decline in sales or profit margin. Following a successful run in the Growth Phase we identify this challenge as a short-lived problem. We believe that this is probably event or economic driven, and it will likely correct itself next quarter, next year, or as we overcome the event or weather the economic storm.

The fact is, often this is the wrong diagnosis. While an event or the economy may have brought the challenges to the forefront, they may not be the underlying cause. Management that falls into the "Denial Trap" fails to fully investigate the problem and relies upon simple answers. In other words, they're denying that another problem may really exist. Deny it too long and you may not be able to recover. If waiting for the problem to go away is one of your top 5 strategies, it's a problem.

LIFE CYCLE TRAPS - SUMMARY

Recognizing where we are in the Business Life Cycle and understanding the traps that plague the various phases can help us avoid the business survival challenges that overtake so many companies. Why is this important to bankability? If you and your management team exhibit an ability to identify, react to, and successfully orchestrate through these phases, it builds confidence in the investors or bankers funding the operation and its growth. Without their trust and confidence, access to capital diminishes.

When you're talking to investors or bankers, it's best if you're able to proactively explain challenging times, how they were identified and managed, and what were the results of those efforts. Notice that I mentioned "proactively" in this instruction. Investors and bankers will quickly identify these challenging times in your historical financial information and, if they're doing their job, they will ask for an explanation. As the business owner, you're better off to have provided the explanation before they identify it or ask. This will be seen as a positive reflection on management of the business, even if the results weren't perfect or still came in poorly.

You can bet that results would have been significantly worse if you hadn't tried anything to address them. If they did come in worse, because of poor or erroneous assumptions, poor implementation, or conditions that changed faster than your ability to course correct, admit it. Explain the circumstances and how they played out, and what you learned from them. Do not make excuses. Excuses are not explanations. Take ownership for your decisions, the lack thereof, and the results. You own the company and you're responsible for how it performs.

CHAPTER 5
VARIOUS TYPES OF CAPITAL
AS A SOURCE OF CASH

You might be wondering, "Why have a section on Types of Capital?" if the focus of this book is on bankability, access to general bank financing. There are numerous forms of capital that can be accessed by businesses. Understanding of these various forms of capital when they are used, and what general characteristics they have, provides for a clear perspective on the requirements of bankability.

Capital is technically defined as the result of subtracting all outside liabilities from all company assets. In essence, it's the equity evidenced on the company balance sheet. The three major types of capital include: working capital, equity capital, and debt capital.

Working capital is the liquid assets available for satisfying the daily operational costs of the company. Essentially, working capital amounts to the company's current assets minus its current liabilities or, from another perspective their accounts receivables plus inventory minus their accounts payable. Again, it's a measure of the company's short-term liquidity; its ability to cover financial obligations. This is why many people interchange, sometimes inappropriately, the terms capital with liquidity.

Equity capital is generated from investors in exchange for ownership in the company. This type of capital can be provided through the sale of stock in the public or private investment markets. In non-stock companies' owners can provide equity capital by contributing cash to the organization.

Debt capital is generated when the company borrows money for operations or investment in assets. Because debt capital has a repayment requirement to the creditor it is evidenced with an offsetting liability on the balance sheet. Established companies generally borrow from financial institutions or the issuance of bonds. Smaller and/or younger businesses may need to rely upon friends and family, credit cards, or government programs to obtain debt capital. This is typically a critical component for businesses. If it doesn't get out of hand it's a great opportunity for businesses to grow and expand.

Some capital types, but not all, are identified below with the Business Life Cycle Phase with which they are most often associated. Each form of capital comes with different requirements, expectations, and cost. I've provided information on the forms of capital in a broad and general sense. A detailed explanation on the various forms of capital and how they're used in business would justify an entire book all by itself. But, understanding where General Bank Financing fits in helps business owners better understand why banks approach your request for bank loans the way they do.

TYPES OF CAPITAL
AND WHEN TO USE THEM

OWNER
CONTRIBUTIONS

FRIENDLY
INVESTOR
OR LENDERS

VENTURE CAPITAL

SPECIALTY
FINANCING

GENERAL BANK FINANCING
STRUCTURED FINANCING
EQUITY INVESTORS

LEARNING	GROWTH	DECLINE/MATURE
PHASE	PHASE	PHASE

Now, let's take a quick look at these various forms of capital, starting with **Owner Contributions**. When a business is starting out, in the Learning Phase, they tend to be fairly high risk. Remember, early on we indicated that many businesses don't survive beyond five years. Some statistics indicate that the failure rate is as high, or higher, than 50%.

Business owners should always be the investor willing to take the most risk. They're betting on themselves, and they intend to get great rewards for taking this risk. As a matter of fact, the return they get on their investment is virtually unlimited. But so is the risk of loss. If they're not willing to do that, it's likely better that they seek their income from a wage earning career as opposed to business ownership.

Therefore, they typically provide the first source of capital (cash) injected into the start of a business. Most outside investors are not willing to take the risk because owners generally aren't willing, or able, to provide them the return they would expect. Therefore, the cost to obtain investor capital could be exorbitant.

As the business begins earning a net profit, owners may also invest the retained earnings from business operations back into the capital need of the business.

As owners begin to exhaust their funds, they often turn to **Friendly Investors or Lenders** that will generally be willing to take on a higher risk as well. These individuals may be family, relatives, co-workers, or close colleagues or friends that have access to investable funds. These people know you personally. They have an emotional and/or professional bond with you. They know you well and have confidence in your ability to make this business venture work. In other words, they're willing to take a higher degree of risk with uncertain returns than other investors.

If you're looking for examples of what the next level of investors looks like, watch the TV series "Shark Tank." While it's clearly a made-for-television version of the process, look at the fundamentals of what is happening. The business owners coming in are looking for an investment. They typically have already used their personal savings, and sometimes, the "friends and family" investors. Now they need additional capital (cash) to grow their company and are asking the "Sharks" to invest. Listen to the questions and explanations the Sharks provide to the entrepreneurs. They focus on risk and reward. They are generally trying to determine, "Will I get my money back and what type of return can I expect for taking this risk?" The risk associated with these early stage businesses is relatively high, and because of this risk level, the return expected by the "Shark Tank" investors is high as well. This can be very costly to the business.

This level of investment capital (cash) expects a higher rate of return than conventional financing. You should expect higher interest rates on loans, royalties on sales, and/or a request for immediate or contingent equity (ownership) in the business. There is a wide variety of loan or investment structures applied at this level, but rest assured, it will come with a price commensurate with the early Growth Phase risk. While the show sometimes shows the success stories around these investments, what they don't show you are the failures, where the "Sharks" lost all or some of their money because things didn't go as planned. The "Sharks" provide **Venture Capital** and **Specialty Financing** in the early Growth Phase of the Business Life Cycle.

As the business begins to successfully perform in the Growth Phase, they typically become eligible for **General Bank Financing**. Remember, banks are responsible for protecting the public's money that was deposited into the bank. Evidence of successful performance by the business indicates that the risk level is now becoming appropriate for the use of those deposits. Sometimes bank financing can be pushed back into the riskier stages of the business by utilizing guaranteed loans through the Small Business Administration (SBA) or other government enhanced lending programs.

In these programs the Small Business Administration assumes a portion of the risk allowing the bank to provide the funding with a limited risk of loss. For instance, business operating loans can be provided through a bank using the SBA 7A Program. The SBA 7A program does not provide the borrower any funds, but guarantees a percentage of any loss taken by the bank, should that occur. These guarantees can be as high as 90% depending upon the circumstances and programs utilized. For instance, with this SBA program a bank could provide a $100,000 loan to a business to cover operating costs. If the business fails and the business assets are sold for $20,000 there would typically be a loss to the bank of $80,000. However, with the SBA 90% guarantee, the bank would only lose $8,000 because 90% of the $80,000 loss ($72,000) is repaid to the bank by the SBA. This significant reduction in risk of loss encourages the bank to loan to businesses with a higher risk than they would without the SBA guarantee.

The SBA 504 program offers support for businesses to acquire funding through banks for the purchase of equipment and real estate. In the SBA 504 program, the borrower provides 10% equity, the SBA provides 40% with a second lien on the assets, and the bank provides 50% of the financing with a first lien on the assets. This reduces the risk to the bank so that they are willing to provide the funds.

Let's look at an example. Let's say a borrower wants to borrow money to purchase a building valued at $1,000,000 for their business. In the SBA 504 program, the borrower must provide $100,000 (10%) towards the purchase, leaving $900,000 yet to be financed. The SBA effectively provides a loan for $400,000 to be applied to the purchase, and the bank provides a loan for the remaining $500,000. Because the bank has a first lien on the building, should the business fail and the building is sold, the bank loan will get repaid first. The SBA loan will get repaid second, and the owner will receive any remaining proceeds from the sale. Therefore, if the building sells for 50% of its original value the bank is fully repaid. A very low risk position for the bank.

Other organizations and states usually offer programs that bridge risk gap between early stage financing sources and conventional bank financing. The structures and terms associated with these programs can prove to be greatly beneficial to the borrower.

Structured Financing is a form of lending that has unique characteristics, such as specific inventory controls, accounts receivable management, and detailed frequent reporting around the current assets of the business and borrowed funds. Larger banks may provide this type of lending and it is typically used throughout the Growth Phase. This is when the demand on cash is high and the assets of the company are heavily weighted to the production cycle of inventory, receivables, and cash needed for operating costs. This funding is necessary to finance the gap between production and receipts from sales.

The final form of capital we have listed is **Equity Capital**. We mentioned equity (ownership) in the Venture and Specialty Financing section where it was required as a way to control the risks associated with the business. Here, the Equity Capital reference is approached differently. In the early stage of the company equity (ownership) is required to protect the investors interest. It allows them an opportunity to share in the success and afford them some level of control or input at the management level if risk begins to increase. In the Growth and Decline or Mature Phases of the cycle, Equity Capital is a friendlier form of capital.

This Equity Capital is provided through stock purchase investors that want to share in the success of the company through ownership; they recognize that the risk is reasonable and therefore expect more reasonable returns. Meanwhile, their management input is generally associated with the election of, and interaction with, the Board of Directors, Chief Executive Officers and Chief Financial Officers of the company. While they may suggest alternative directions for the company, they do not typically directly control the company actions.

This form of Equity Capital can be provided to publicly traded companies, those where one can purchase ownership through the public stock exchanges, or privately held companies where investors contribute to the organization's capital position in exchange for an equity ownership position.

There are numerous financing structures used by businesses that combine or overlap those described above. Suffice it to say, capital for a business may be provided through a variety of available cash sources, including retained earnings, debt, and/or equity. You may have run across the term "Capital Stack." The "Capital Stack" for any company is a rank ordering of the types of capital provided to a company from various sources. The "Stack" refers to the rank ordering of these sources by the level of risk, return, and repayment priority associated with each.

I have covered these capital types in a broad and general sense in order to help you better understand where general bank financing fits in the Business Life Cycle and to present the relationship between risk and reward expected by various levels of capital providers.

CHAPTER 6
ECONOMIC CHANGE –
WHAT HAPPENS?

Bankability changes with the economic conditions. By describing what happens within businesses and banks during tough economic times, you will gain an appreciation for how to prepare and successfully navigate through them.

When the economy takes a turn for the worse, business becomes challenging for everyone. Depending upon the cause of the economic downturn, some industries may be impacted more than others. Take for instance the recession of 2007-09. This recession was driven by the financial sector over-extending credit into the real estate markets. The willingness to do this started with Congressional authorization for Fannie Mae, the quasi-governmental provider of residential mortgages, to provide mortgages with much riskier terms in order to accelerate home ownership. Therefore, because Fannie Mae and investment bankers were willing to buy these higher risk loans, banks originated them and sold them into the residential mortgage investment market. As more and more risk entered this sector, real estate investors began losing money in a dramatic fashion. While everyone suffered financially to some degree, three sectors got hit the hardest: the real estate sector, the banking sector, and more importantly the home-owner consumer.

For our purposes we need a more general understanding of economic change and the resulting circumstances affecting businesses <u>AND</u> banks. Therefore, we're going to look at four components associated with each. We'll consider the Perspective, Impact, Reactions, and Results on both, businesses and banks. Let's start with the businesses.

BUSINESS OWNER PERSPECTIVE

When these downturns occur, everyone has a perspective based upon the impact they're experiencing. In general, businesses find that credit is tighter. Their perspective tends to be that it's all the banks' fault. You'll hear things like, "Our cash flow is tight, and we need more money" or "The banks won't lend any money and now they're reducing my line of credit." This is a "victim" perspective that is further supported by the news media. The media tends to report this perspective because they don't take the time to understand the entire environment or report on a complete story that includes the reasons the banks won't lend; but the essence of what the business owner is feeling is correct. One of the keys to managing it successfully is understanding the natural conditions of an economic downturn and the reactions to those associated with your business.

BANK PERSPECTIVE

Well, as they say, there are always two sides to every story. That doesn't mean that one is right, and the other is wrong; it just means that there are two perspectives. From the banks' perspective, they're just trying to minimize loss and protect the depositors' money, but the impact of those actions on their business borrowers are evidenced in the business owner's perspective. Banks are not intentionally trying to shut businesses down or discontinue lending. From the banks' perspective, lending risk is increasing due to poor business performance. They begin to see an increasing number of businesses that can't cover their debt service. Due to the potential risk of loss in their loan portfolios, regulators appropriately expect the banks to tighten standards on new loans to compensate for those that are under stress and previously underwritten on normalized cash flows and financial performance.

Shortly after retiring from banking in 2016, I was invited by a business roundtable facilitator to attend his roundtable meeting. I graciously accepted, curious to learn more about how peer group roundtables worked and what value they provided. The roundtable group consisted of eight, what I call, "Community Based" business owners. These businesses are smaller than "Middle Market" but have been in existence for some time and are generally family owned and locally domiciled. This group represented the types of businesses that I worked with for over 35 years.

The facilitator introduced me to the group with a quick description of my career in banking. Shortly after being introduced, one of the business owners, rather bluntly, asked me this, "Given your background in banking, when do you think banks will want to start lending to businesses again?"

Now, you need to recognize that the Great Recession started at the beginning of 2008 and technically lasted until early 2010. Unfortunately, the recovery efforts put forth were lackluster compared to efforts provided in previous, much less severe, recessions. This caused one of the most protracted recoveries ever experienced. It wasn't until early 2016 that businesses and investors began to regain confidence in the future economy and reinvest in business growth. As this question was posed to me in early 2017, it was founded in over eight years of economic downturn and an extremely sluggish recovery. There was a lot of frustration in the business and banking communities.

So, back to the question. Following a slight pause for thought I responded with a question for the business owner. I asked, "Presuming that you produce goods or services for sale, how often do you produce these goods or services and essentially put them on the shelf without an effort to sell them?" His response, as expected, was that that would be foolish. I agreed, and then went on to explain that his original question was essentially asking me the same thing. I further explained that banks "always" want to make loans to businesses. If they didn't, they'd likely go broke, just like a business that doesn't want to sell their products or services.

Remembering the previous explanation of banking from the chapter "How Banking Works and Why it Matters," we should be able to conclude that a bank that is paying interest and insurance premiums on deposits, coupled with operational costs, would need to loan out the deposits in order to generate enough interest income to sustain operations. The problem isn't in the banks' fundamental desire to loan money, it's in their desire to limit risk in a high risk environment. In essence, fewer businesses now qualify for "risk appropriate" loans from the bank.

The banks are caught in a "Catch-22." If they increase their lending activity too much, through an increased appetite for risk, and things don't quickly improve, their problems are exacerbated, and they'll likely experience regulatory actions and/or failure. If, on the other hand, they don't loan enough money, they won't generate the earnings necessary to maintain financial viability.

As a business owner, think about it like this: You have several customers that are key contributors to your annual sales volume. During a recession, they become significantly slow to pay. Then one of them fails to pay altogether and your product or service is gone. It's just a straight up loss. As you work to replace these weak clients, do you accept anybody? Or do you try to find financially stable operators on whom you can rely for purchases and payment?

It's this dynamic that drives the perception that banks don't want to lend. They want to lend. They just end up in the same scenario as any other business. They must figure out how to conduct business in a risk appropriate, regulatory compliant, and profitable manner when the risks associated with their potential borrowers has increased significantly.

CHAPTER 7
HOW TOUGH ECONOMIC ENVIRONMENTS AFFECT BUSINESSES

BUSINESS OWNER IMPACT

Economic downturns can have a dramatic impact on businesses. What tends to make them so dramatic is that they impact the business on several fronts. Let's look at a few. One of the first things businesses notice is a reduction in revenue. In essence, demand for the product or service is falling. The orders are getting smaller in size and less frequent. New customer acquisition is difficult, at best, as everyone is experiencing these conditions and competition is heating up.

With more aggressive competition, customers begin demanding lower prices which essentially compresses your margins, exacerbating the problems caused by a reduction in revenue.

If you're in a business that inventories product for future orders, your inventories grow, creating an oversupply in the market and a consumption of the increasingly valuable resource of cash. The inventory build-up is a result of ordering and production adjustments lagging sales.

Since everyone is experiencing similar conditions you may also begin experiencing increased costs. These cost increases could manifest themselves in the purchase of raw materials where you don't have alternative sources, service and product suppliers that have cost escalation clauses in your agreements, or interest rates on term or operating debt. All of these impacts are creating a demand on cash.

BUSINESS OWNER REACTION

Since we all know that cash flow is the very lifeblood of any business organization, most businesses quickly look to their operating lines of credit to supplement deficient cash flows. Depending upon the terms and conditions on your line of credit, this may or may not be a viable short term solution to cash deficiencies. If company cash and/or the line of credit can't supply the necessary operating cash, credit cards get used, payments get delayed, work schedules get reduced, and other cost reductions are implemented.

The quicker you can reduce production, labor, and other costs to match sales, the better you're able to minimize this impact. Most business owners appropriately go through a period of analysis to determine the cause for the loss of sales. This may be followed by an unfortunate period of denial or a belief that it's a short-lived circumstance, or a problem with a few customer orders.

As last resorts, businesses will look for additional cash through the sale of assets, high-priced loans, or investor capital. The sale of assets may include the bulk sale of inventory at discounted prices, the sale of an operating division, or even the sale of fixed assets, such as real estate or equipment. Keep in mind that asset sales in a challenged economy will be difficult to achieve.

BUSINESS OWNER RESULT

The result of all this activity, internal and external, is generally exhibited in poor financial performance. Here's a quick summary of what you can expect to happen to your financial performance in an economic downturn. As we mentioned previously, cash flow slows down or even turns negative and you attempt to reduce the cash flow disparity from numerous sources. Your liquidity (cash on hand) declines limiting you from implementing certain corrective measures that require additional cash. The business' ability to make debt payments diminishes as less cash is available after operating expenses are paid.

If losses occur, the strength of your balance sheet is impaired as earnings decline and will show up in a higher debt-to-net worth ratio. If you are able to borrow additional money to support operations, the increase in debt will further weaken your balance sheet position. Further damage can result from the discounted sale of assets.

Through all of this, the most notable result is that profitability declines or goes negative, causing loan covenant defaults and a further tightening of available loan funds needed for survival. All of these impacts have a negative effect on your bankability. As you fight through all these challenges, there just doesn't seem to be any solution in sight.

CHAPTER 8
HOW TOUGH ECONOMIC
ENVIRONMENTS AFFECT BANKS

BANK IMPACT

One of the first impacts to a bank in times of economic stress is reduced revenues. However, it's interesting to note that, unlike other businesses, it isn't from a reduced demand. As a matter of fact, the demand for loans is probably at a high point. The problem is due to the risk imposed into businesses and the market generating fewer lending opportunities. Remember when I said banks are always willing to lend, but at a certain risk level? Their reduction in revenues is from the lack of risk appropriate opportunities coupled with intense competition for the qualifying loan opportunities.

This is a windfall for businesses that are well prepared for the economic downturn. The ability to negotiate lower rates and more flexible terms when you're a strong, qualified borrower in tough times is significantly improved over normal times.

Banks also experience a challenge in reducing inventory, not unlike that of businesses. The banks' inventory is the deposits we discussed previously. It's the cost of those deposits that influences the cost of funds (cost of goods sold) at the bank.

It's very awkward, if not plain difficult, and probably foolish, to ask depositors to take their money out of the bank. Lowering interest paid on deposits is only an option for time deposits (savings and money market accounts or certificates of deposit, etc.) and even then, the strategy is flawed. Every bank competitor is doing the same thing essentially, trying to reduce deposit costs. Therefore, inventory cost remains relatively stable while revenue generating loan balances decline and new loan originations are generated at lower interest rates.

Furthermore, since deposits are not being used for lending, they are used to purchase other income producing investments, like treasury bills, bonds, loan pools, etc. These investments generally generate earnings at a lower rate than organically generated loans. All of these factors create margin compression.

But there's another, even greater, impact experienced by banks. In the event that a business fails or enters bankruptcy, the bank will likely lose, not just some interest earnings from the loan, but some or all of the loan itself. (That was the depositors' money.) To replace that money, the bank has to take it from earnings.

So, let's do a little math. Let's say the bank loses $1,000,000 on a loan that isn't repaid and that they operate on a 3.5% margin. In order for the bank to earn enough money to replace that loss over the next year, they would need to loan out an additional $28,571,428 ($1,000,000/.035) for 12 months. That's a tall order in a tough economy where risk appropriate loans are hard to come by and competition is fierce.

As banks are challenged to generate risk appropriate income at lower margins, just like businesses, they begin to experience increased costs. At a bank, during an economic downturn, costs rise in servicing existing loans, collections and problem loan workouts, loan losses, and new loan originations. As with a business, cost reductions lag loan originations and add to the burden of excess cost compared to revenue generated. Bankers also go through a period of analysis to determine the cause for the decrease in loan originations, typically followed by an unfortunate period of denial or a belief that it's a short-lived circumstance or a problem with a few potential prospects.

BANK REACTION

Once the bank acknowledges that they are entering a challenging economic environment they immediately increase borrower monitoring. Their efforts include reviewing the financial performance of the business borrowers. This may involve a review of existing financial information on past borrower business performance and/or a request for updated and more frequent reporting of financial performance by the borrower. They begin to watch the timeliness of payments made and the compliance with loan covenants. If either of these begin to falter, they will be quick to engage in a conversation with the borrower to determine if adjustments need to be made in order to limit the risk of loss to the bank.

Based on these considerations, the bank will begin to develop contingency plans for sustainability. One must remember that, for the bank, this isn't just about one customer having a problem, this is about virtually all their customers having a problem. They will develop risk tolerance levels by industry and review lending standards to ensure that new loan originations do not add to the problem. This essentially reduces credit availability to the general business community.

As all this is going on, the bank will increase or accelerate collection activity. Keeping loan payments current throughout a recession is critical to the survival of the business and the bank. If the business cannot keep the loan payments current, the bank will look for a quick solution because there is another loan having problems coming up right behind the loan they're working on.

Like businesses, banks will look for ways to reduce costs through staff reductions, production costs, and operational purchases. They will also, as we discussed above, attempt to reduce interest paid on deposits.

As challenges continue, they may look to asset sales as well. One type of asset sale would involve the sale of problem loans at a discount to the buyer. This effectively achieves two things. First, it reduces the risk of loss in the bank's loan portfolio. Second, since there is a regulatory expectation that problem loans do not reach levels that could impair the bank's survival, it provides room in the problem loan portfolio for other loans experiencing problems without causing regulatory concern.

The banks may also engage in the sale of hard assets. First, any assets they have acquired through the loan workout process (real estate, equipment, inventory, etc.) and second, the sale of bank assets such as branch offices. This may take place as a branch operation sale that includes the deposits and loans of the branch offered for sale or it could be a sale of a banking facility with an agreement with the buyer to lease the facility back for continued bank operations.

BANK RESULT

So, what do we think the result of all this has been on the bank? It really isn't that much different than the effect on other businesses. First and foremost, they begin to experience poor financial performance. Loan quality deteriorates as evidenced through increases in loan covenant defaults, payment delinquency, collection costs, and loan losses. Through all of this, profitability declines, and if severe enough, may actually go negative.

During this time, banks are aggressively seeking risk appropriate borrowers to compensate for the weak performing borrowers being generated by the economic stress. In the face of fierce competition, banks are challenged to acquire these risk appropriate borrowers once they're found. Well performing borrowers do not like to change banking relationships in the middle of tough economic times. There's too much uncertainty around how the new bank would manage their relationship. In order to entice these borrowers to move or bring business to the bank, the bank will likely offer lower interest rates, more flexible loan terms and performance conditions.

While these enticements might make sense at the time they're offered, they effectively set the bank up for potential problems down the road. The concessions offered will outlive the economic downturn, and the bank will have built in a degree of lower margined loans with weaker risk management structures that potentially exacerbate existing loan quality issues in their loan portfolio.'

THE PERFECT STORM

We've just described a scenario that sounds like the perfect storm. If you've read the book, or seen the movie "The Perfect Storm," you realize that all the environmental conditions existed to create a storm beyond all expectations. In the story, the storm doesn't just affect some boats, it affects all boats. How well each boat survives the storm is dependent upon how well built and prepared it is to handle the stress coupled with how well the captain and crew react to the conditions they encounter. Sometimes, no matter how good we are, or how strong the boat, the circumstances are overwhelming, and we sink.

But, in business, there are a lot of things you can do to prepare for such an event that will provide you with the best odds for survival, if not an opportunity to further your success. While no one wants to encounter this perfect storm, there are few reasons that you can't be prepared to respond appropriately. This requires a matter of perspective during good times that becomes even more useful in tough times. Let's take a look at how you can prepare your businesses for tough times.

CHAPTER 9

A MATTER OF PERSPECTIVE –
PREPARING FOR TOUGH TIMES

The mindset of the business owner is directly correlated to the quality and effectiveness of business management. With the right mindset, owners position their businesses for greater levels of success. Banks will factor this into the assessment of bankability. Here's a great way to think about the impact of your perspective.

The concept is called, "The Three Eyes of the Entrepreneur."[1] This illustration is used to help business owners understand the value of perspective. Studies have shown that in a typical operating environment the business owner has three perspectives that get applied to running the business.

---

[1] "The Three Eyes of the Entrepreneur" as presented by Brian Tracy through FocalPoint Coaching, Inc.

3 EYES OF THE ENTREPRENEUR

The Managerial Eye is looking backwards. Managers look at results, something that has already happened. They look at financial performance reports, sales activity, production results, delivery times, etc. All these things have already happened, and the manager is checking to see if they meet expectations. If they don't, managers can then apply appropriate course corrections, assuming they understand the Entrepreneurial perspective. The third eye in the diagram is the Technician's Eye. You'll notice that the technician's eyes look a little bloodshot. That's because they are always looking down at the work at hand. The technician represents the worker performing daily tasks, working at their desk, on the line, or in the field to accomplish specific tasks necessary for the business to operate.

Most owners of small to medium sized businesses (SMB's) spend the majority, sometimes up to 80% or more, of their time in the Technician's role. They might spend 30 – 50% of their time in the Manager's role and 30% or less in the Entrepreneurial role. As you look at the diagram, you'll notice a value/hour indication for each perspective. This represents an approximate salary level for each role, with the Entrepreneurial role having a virtually unlimited value, as it is determined by the success of the organization.

From this information, the business owner can essentially calculate an indication of their value contribution to the business. If the business owner spends most of their time in a Technician role, they don't bring much value. We could probably hire someone to take on those responsibilities for much less than the company is paying the owner. By now, you should get the general idea of this representation. But there's more to understand.

It has been suggested that 80% of all business success is driven out of the Entrepreneur's and Manager's perspectives. This doesn't mean that the Technician doesn't add significant value to the operation. Certainly, without them we wouldn't have much of a business, if we would have one at all. But the decisions that are driven out of the Manager and Entrepreneurial perspectives are what really moves the business forward. What's even more interesting is that out of the 80% contribution, 80% of it comes from the Entrepreneur's perspective and 20% from the Manager's perspective. For those mathematicians out there, that means the Entrepreneurial perspective contributes 64%, or virtually 2/3rds, to the overall success of the organization.

Now, if you're the business owner, where are you spending your time? Where should you be spending your time? And what is your real value contribution? Ask yourself: Are you spending 3+ days each week working from an entrepreneurial perspective?

Why is this important to our discussion around bankability? The business owner's perspective drives the behaviors of the organization. If they are focused on tomorrow, they will ensure that the organization is appropriately prepared for good times and bad. If they have their head down at the desk or are tied up in daily tasks, they'll likely never see the change coming until it's too late, or they'll casually see it and procrastinate addressing it due all the demands of functioning as a technician.

During a perfect storm environment, you'll likely need to use all three eyes to manage through the situation, but pay particular attention to the Entrepreneurial Eye. You will need this perspective to guide you out of the challenges. Think about it this way. If you're looking at the hood ornament on a car while driving, how well would you navigate the curves and turns of the road?

Here's another matter of perspective for both business owners and bankers - Transactions vs. Relationships. Most businesses gauge their opinion of their banking arrangement based on the timeliness of handling their lending needs and getting the lowest possible interest rate. And most lenders gauge the relationship on "winning" the deal and compliance with bank policy and lending terms.

How do you look at your banking arrangement? Do you see your relationship with bankers as a transactional negotiation for your loan approval or renewal? Bankers, do you value your success on "winning the deal?" Typically, the honest answers to these questions are, yes. With these perspectives the banking activity is reduced to a "Transactional' perspective. In and of itself that may not be a bad perspective, however, there's a lot more at stake between the bank and the business than "winning" the transactional negotiation. When a business relies upon a bank to provide cash for operations or expansion, it shouldn't be about a transaction. And when a bank offers to provide cash to a business, it should do so with a deeper understanding of the value of an ongoing relationship.

Why? Because businesses need cash, and banks need loans, in both good times and bad. Quality banking relationships transcend good times and bad. They last throughout both, because both parties work together to ensure that they will.

This is a crucial perspective. Consider it from a different vantage point. Instead of a bank, let's assume the business has gone to a successful investor to acquire investor funding instead of bank funding. The investor is likely to desire a close relationship with the business in order to understand the ongoing risks associated with their investment. They won't likely look at this as a transaction, but rather an ongoing relationship of understanding and support. The value of a deeper understanding found in a relationship far exceeds that of a transaction and elicits continued support, even throughout challenging times.

The banker must have the business owner's success as a priority. They need to ensure that they intrinsically understand the borrower's business at a level where they understand the risks associated with the continued operation of the business and the ability to anticipate future capital needs for operations and/or expansion in both good times and bad. Having this understanding, it is their responsibility to work with the business owner such that both parties understand the potential impacts the business may encounter and the expected requirements necessary to secure or maintain funding in those scenarios. In other words, the banker is looking after the success of the business because they value the ongoing relationship, not the transaction. It provides a value to both parties. This approach lowers the risk of loss and increases the opportunity for success for the bank and the borrower.

The same is true for the business owner. As a business owner, would you treat an investor or partner with the same transactional indifference you apply to your bank borrowing activity? If you did, your access to funds would likely be limited quickly. If you want the advantages of a banking relationship that remains supportive in tough times, you need to understand the needs of the banking institution and how they relate to the current and future success of your business. Bankability can be considered a success barometer for your business. If your business is structured and managed to be bankable through good times and bad, you will have a positive relationship with your bank, access to capital, and confidence that your business will survive during difficult times. What a great, low cost insurance policy.

CHAPTER 10
THE FIVE Cs OF CREDIT

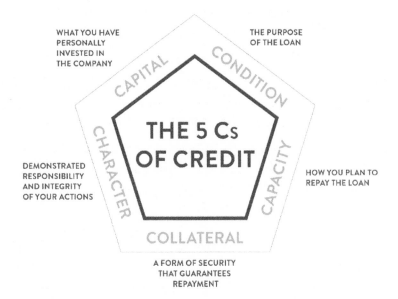

WHAT YOU HAVE
PERSONALLY
INVESTED IN
THE COMPANY

THE PURPOSE
OF THE LOAN

CAPITAL

CONDITION

THE 5 Cs OF CREDIT

CHARACTER

CAPACITY

DEMONSTRATED
RESPONSIBILITY
AND INTEGRITY
OF YOUR ACTIONS

HOW YOU PLAN TO
REPAY THE LOAN

COLLATERAL

A FORM OF SECURITY
THAT GUARANTEES
REPAYMENT

That brings us to the Five 5 Cs of credit. Early in their banking career, bankers are taught the Five Cs of credit as an introductory way to determine appropriate risk and bankability of loan applicants. While these are frequently shared in a generic form, they are seldom presented with a deeper understanding of what they should look like and why they have meaning. As you can see in the graphic, the descriptions are generic in nature and transaction focused. Measuring the strength of each of these characteristics at a deeper level allows the lender to assess risk, but the words themselves tell us little about the underlying assessment. Therefore, we're going to discuss these further and determine how they relate to or manifest themselves in the business and banking environments.

These Five Cs represent the core of bankability. If you get nothing else from this book, be sure to take away a strong understanding of these five critical components of lending. From my perspective, the Five Cs are not created equal, and there is a priority to the way they are perceived and interpreted by bankers. Here's how I would rank them from most important to least:

1) Character
2) Capacity
3) Capital
4) Collateral
5) Conditions

I look at the first three as the sides of a triangle. A triangle is one of the strongest geometric shapes and can withstand significant stress. The stronger you are in character, capacity, and capital, the less reliance the bank needs to put on collateral and conditions. Companies that exhibit the strongest levels in these three components virtually render the other two irrelevant. That's the "Holy Grail." When you achieve that, you represent the best in bankability.

Typically, the bank only relies upon repayment from the sale of collateral when operating profits cannot satisfy the debt service obligations. That exception occurs when the bank provides operating capital where repayment is directly supported by the sale of revenue-generating assets. If the capacity and capital of the borrower is strong, their reliance on the sale of non-revenue generating assets for repayment is diminished.

The definition for conditions includes numerous factors that are outside of the borrower's control. The purpose of this book is to help you position your company for bankability under a variety of conditions. Most of that effort is focused on the first three Cs: Character, Capacity, and Capital. Let's start with "Character."

CHARACTER

> *Watch your thoughts, they become your words; watch your words, they become your actions; watch your actions, they become your habits; watch your habits, they become your character; watch your character, it becomes your destiny.*
>
> *Lao Tzu, Ancient Chinese Philosopher*

Lao Tzu lived between the 4th and 6th centuries BC, when apparently the definition of character was an important topic, and I think, this quote sums up character better than any I've found. As he indicates, one's character is exhibited through a person's thoughts, words, and actions.

Currently, Character is defined in the <u>Cambridge Dictionary</u> as "the particular combination of qualities in a person or place that makes them different from others," but it's obviously more than that. The phrase "good character" was most popular in the 19th century. Warren Susman in his book, <u>Culture as History</u>, indicates that in those times, "character" was a keyword of Englishmen and Americans and was promoted as an essential component of one's identity.

Susman points out that the 20th century brought about a different perspective. Society had transitioned from a producing society, to a consuming society, to one where our focus shifted from virtue and goodness to one of self and material possessions. As Susman puts it, "The vision of self-sacrifice began to yield to that of self-realization." Cultivating one's personality traits, influence, and perception by others became more important than developing the nobility of one's feelings, thoughts, and actions.

Today, the term "Character" is frequently used and seldom defined in the context of circumstances or expectations. But, in general, we think of it as the notable traits of a person, sometimes referring to moral excellence or firmness. A true definition can prove to be somewhat elusive. In one case I found a list of over 400 traits related to one's character. Another article I researched referenced as many as 800. Therefore, what do we really mean when we use "Character" as one of the Five Cs?

I think it's obvious that we'd be looking for positive traits. Traits that would support the expectations of the lender, evidence strong leadership, and contribute to the success of the business enterprise. This could be interpreted to mean that the borrower or business owner does the right things for the right reasons because they believe it's morally right to do so, has a good history of performance, and is trustworthy and honest.

Life experience teaches us that functioning with good character improves one's self-esteem, relationships, and satisfaction with life in general. Exhibiting good character traits fosters respect and trust from others, while motivating those around us to be better as well. These good character traits, supported and developed by our values, help us establish a framework upon which to make important decisions and choices. This, in turn, builds our self-confidence and respect. Our good character traits provide an indication of our ability to lead and be successful, both personally and professionally.

So, in the context of a banking relationship, what does "Character" really mean, and how is it exhibited? If we ask a group of businesspeople to provide words that describe a good person's character, we're likely to hear things like: Responsible, Honest, Successful, Organized, Leader, etc. A banker would agree that these are worthy traits and desirable in the lending relationship. Bankers would likely group character traits into three categories, 1.) those that evidence high moral standards, 2.) those that support strong management and leadership ability, and 3.) those that contribute to overcoming adversity and capitalizing on opportunity.

For the purpose of staying focused on bankability, I selected five character traits that I believe would be most meaningful to a lender. Anytime we speak about character traits we'll find overlapping definitions, but as we explore each one more deeply, you'll see some distinct differences. After we've reviewed all five, you'll have a clearer picture of what "Good Character" looks like in a banking relationship. Let's take a look at each.

1.) **Integrity** – This word is afforded broad interpretation when discussed as a character trait. Often being used interchangeably with honesty. The root of the word Integrity means "whole" or "undivided." A person with integrity does not act one way in one situation and another way in a similar situation. Exhibiting integrity builds trust in others and is shown through strong moral principles and core values. A person with integrity conducts their life and makes decisions founded in their moral principles and core values, and it doesn't matter if their conduct or decisions are evident to others.

Bankers look for someone that has strong moral principles and core values that they can trust and rely upon in difficult situations. Bankers want borrowers that are true to themselves and their word, even when faced with difficult consequences for the commitments they've made. Borrowers with integrity are not compromised by the consequences of their actions. They stay consistent, regardless of how awkward the situation may be.

Individuals with integrity allow their decisions and actions to represent who they are and what they believe in. Which brings us to the second Character Trait.

2.) **Honesty** – As previously mentioned, the terms 'Honesty' and 'Integrity' are frequently, and inaccurately, considered synonyms and used interchangeably. They may not be identical twins, but they are closely related and in the same family. Honesty is about telling the truth. Not just to others, but most importantly, to yourself. You see, if you can't be honest with yourself, you'll have no problem at all being dishonest with others. And Honesty isn't just about what you say, it's about being authentic in such a way that others can depend upon you to be straightforward and trustworthy.

Dishonesty includes the omission of salient information and facts, providing outright inaccurate information, not following laws and rules while justifying it through some fictitious offsetting excuse, and agreeing to do things while knowing you have no intention of following through. You see, Honesty is about living the truth in a way that allows you to be trustworthy in all your relationships, interactions, and thoughts.

So, if being dishonest, even a little, can cause so much damage, why do people lie? It seems to me that most people lie because they are scared of what will happen if they tell the truth, or they are trying to hide something because they believe it provides them an advantage of some kind.

We've all heard the saying, "Honesty is the best policy." Logically, it's the only way to be if you intend to be successful. If you're not honest with others, you'll destroy the trust they have in you, and trust is exceedingly difficult to regain once lost. Even if an individual knows that you've been dishonest with others, while you're being honest with them, you'll lose credibility and trust.

Here's a quick banking example. I had a business owner approach me at the bank for a business loan, the details of which are irrelevant. What is relevant is that as we were conducting our due diligence, we found that the business income statements had significant differences from what was reported on their tax return. Now, typically, these two documents don't match exactly due to differences between the Generally Accepted Accounting Principles (GAAP) applied to the preparation of income statements and the Internal Revenue Service (IRS) laws and regulations used in the preparation of taxes.

However, when the differences cannot be easily reconciled, it calls into question the accuracy of the documents. When I asked the borrower to explain the differences, they informed me that a significant amount of their business was conducted in cash transactions that they didn't report on their taxes.

Even though they were being honest with me, they weren't being honest with the IRS. Once I knew this, I found it difficult to trust them. If they can justify lying to the IRS, when will they start lying to me. Needless to say, we didn't make the loan.

Bankers don't have a deep knowledge of the loan applicants prior to the loan request. So how do they gauge the integrity and honesty of the applicant? At times, this can be difficult. Credit Bureau Reports (CBR's) are a starting point. Evidence of slow payments, charge offs, or bankruptcy may be the start of concerns. Getting a truthful story behind these events helps the banker to identify integrity and honesty traits. The interview process in itself provides certain insights, and consistency in year-over-year financial reporting coupled with honest explanations will definitely lead the lender to a degree of comfort or discomfort with the applicant's integrity and honesty.

It can be an inexact science, but it's critical that the lender feel comfortable with the integrity and honesty of the applicant. If the applicant demonstrates these two primary character traits, the lender begins to look at Responsibility.

3.) **Responsibility** - This character trait encompasses a broad array of behavioral descriptions and has significant impacts on the perception of your character. So, what does it mean to be responsible or take responsibility? This is one of those things where you know it when you see it, but it's difficult to describe, so bear with me as I try to frame this in an understandable way.

First and foremost, I would say that a responsible person is dependable. When they agree to do something, they do it. They understand the burden of obligation and the duty they have to perform. They realize that if they let people down, they'll stop believing in them. They recognize that we all rely upon others for our success and they do everything in their power to follow through on their commitments. Doing this consistently allows others to take you seriously and rely upon your commitments.

In addition, they hold themselves accountable. They don't make excuses or blame others or circumstances for poor results. They recognize that the buck stops with them and they are accountable to others. In acknowledging this, they don't complain, they admit their mistakes, accept the responsibility for their actions and the need to correct things when necessary.

This incorporates a willingness to take ownership for their decisions and actions. They don't rely upon others to remind them what they are supposed to do or where they are supposed to be. They take ownership for being prepared and on time. If they need to cancel something, they do so as soon as possible. To ensure things happen as intended, they are well organized in everything they do.

We couldn't discuss the character trait of Responsibility without mentioning that responsible individuals are trustworthy. They recognize that trust needs to be earned, and therefore, takes an effort on their part. As we mentioned in Honesty, they adhere to telling the truth to earn and maintain the trust of others. Those with a strong Responsibility trait know that if someone trusts them to take care of something, perform at a certain level, or maintain something in confidence, they must do it. It's important to them that others can count on them.

Thinking things through and the use of good judgement is a key piece of being responsible. When you think things through you make better choices. This indicates to others that they can trust your decisions. Using good judgement, responsible individuals respect authority and follow the rules.

Being a responsible person means that you are respectful of others. You recognize that virtually all your efforts affect or are connected to the needs of others. Therefore, when you have a job to do, you do it, and you do it on time. By being self-disciplined, you don't procrastinate, and you fulfill your obligations with care and consideration for others.

Banks use a variety of factors to gauge your level of responsibility. One of the most frequently used methods is reviewing the stability of your company operations and the management of retained earnings. A company with an erratic performance trend may indicate an inability to plan and execute responsibly. If the company has had a good history of profitability but all the retained earnings have been taken, leaving the company undercapitalized, it indicates a lack of fiscal responsibility that puts the financial stability of the company at risk.

Banks also consider past payment performance and evidence that the business owner readily takes ownership of the past performance and results of the company, regardless of whether they are good or bad.

4.) **Reliability** – As with Integrity and Honesty, Responsibility and Reliability are close cousins in the family of Character Traits. Reliability focuses more directly on the fact that others can consistently depend upon you to follow through on your commitments, actions, and decisions. Good patterns of behavior and decision making are evident and predictable to the degree that someone may depend upon your accuracy, honesty, and/or achievement.

From a business perspective these patterns become evident in organizational results over time, instilling confidence that failure is unlikely to occur. Others can consistently depend upon you with a high level of confidence that the expected results will occur within a reasonable variance.

To lend someone money, the banker needs to develop confidence that the financial projections indicating the ability to pay will be achieved. If historical results are erratic, even with reasonable explanation, it will call your Reliability into question.

5.) **Perseverance** – Perseverance is about steadfastly keeping a hard focus on your goals and working diligently to achieve them. It's about never giving up. That doesn't mean that you stay with a plan that isn't working, it means that you focus on the goal and aggressively adapt, when necessary, to ensure that you achieve your objective. It's about persistence and determination, and in many respects, hard work, to continue on the path towards achievement, even when it's difficult or uncomfortable for the sake of reaching your goal or expected outcome.

In business, Perseverance usually isn't the effort of just one person. Typically, it takes a team of people to operate your business successfully. Therefore, in order for you to continue on a course of action in the face of challenges that may indicate minimal possibility of success, you need the entire team to be on board. To effectively do this, you'll need strong communication, leadership, management, and people skills.

From the banker's perspective, it's difficult to assess these skills without the benefit of previous exposure to your business operations. However, they are able to draw some conclusions based upon the degree of effort demonstrated in the business plan presented for your loan request, coupled with the historical performance of the company. Additionally, they will get some indication of your communication skills at the time of loan application and throughout the life of the loan.

This Character Trait is especially important to bankers. They need to know that you are 100+% committed to being successful with whatever the plan is, and you have the ability to lead your team to the achievement of your goals. The repayment of their loan depends upon it.

Before we leave the topic of Character, let's talk a little bit about communication. How your banker interprets your character, or even the risk associated with your business, is greatly influenced by your communication with them. Sure, the financial analysis of the numbers is a major factor, but aside from the numbers, the frequency and quality of your interactions significantly impact their perception and decisions about your company.

These perceptions are impacted by your willingness and ability to correspond throughout the relationship. Regular, proactive communication is the key. The banker shouldn't have to ask you for information you've already agreed to provide. If it's going to be late in its delivery, let the banker know before it's due. If events at your business change in a way that could potentially impact your results, reach out and discuss the changes with your banker. If you only talk with your banker when your loan is up for renewal or when you need additional funding, you're already playing catch up. If your banker doesn't automatically schedule quarterly or semi-annual meetings with you (and they should), take the initiative and schedule meetings with them, preferably at your place of business. Here's a short story about the value of communication.

A prospective client of mine called me one day requesting a discussion about some changes that had occurred in his business. Upon meeting with him, I found out that some significant management responsibility changes he made the previous year weren't working out. The changes had created a material negative impact on the company's sales, revenue, profitability, and cash flow. They were now in a cash crisis. As he provided the details, I became concerned about how the bank providing his operating Line of Credit was going to react. If they reduced his availability to funding on the line, he might not be able to recover. So, I asked the question, "Have you talked with your banker about this?" His response was typical to many business owner's perspective in these situations; he didn't plan on informing his banker until he had this under control.

Wrong answer! I went on to share with him that, 1) the bank was likely already aware of the problem as they monitored the company performance through financial reporting and performance covenants, 2) they were likely waiting to hear from him regarding the course correction plan, and 3) while he may not believe it, the bank would potentially be able to assist in solving the problem if he proactively approached them with an update and a plan.

He was reluctant, but agreed to speak with his banker that afternoon. In a follow up call, after he had met with the banker, I asked if they had restricted his line of credit. He admitted that he had been using the wrong approach. The banker was able to increase the availability on the line of credit, providing access to additional funds, and waived the covenant default for the next two quarters while the business implemented its course corrections. Additionally, they scheduled monthly update meetings going forward to ensure that both were informed of any potential changes and the progress made.

If he had waited, the bank would have declared him in default of the performance covenants and likely would have immediately reduced the availability to funds on the line of credit. Why would they do this? Because by not knowing what the situation was, they are assuming the worst and protecting their ability to recover the depositor's money that was being lent to the business.

Don't ever let your banker be surprised or left in the dark when things aren't going as planned. Be responsible. Proactively communicate with your banker on a regular basis regarding the performance of your business and make a special effort to quickly communicate when things turn the wrong direction.

CAPACITY

Second only to Character, Capacity is the most important of the Five Cs. It doesn't matter what your repayment capacity is if your character is flawed, and you can't be relied upon to meet your obligations. Capacity focuses on your primary source of repayment, cash flow. The focus involves two perspectives. The first, is the adequacy of cash flow to repay the debt, and the second is the risk to the cash flow being relied upon for the repayment of the debt. Collateral isn't taken into consideration here, because it is only liquidated when the borrower fails to repay the loan.

The bank is looking for solid indications that your business has the financial wherewithal to support the operational expenses AND debt repayment. In their efforts to determine the probability of repayment, they'll review Credit Bureau Reports to see the historical pattern of debt repayment. This historical record provides some indication regarding future payment expectations. They will also review a number of financial metrics and calculate a number of financial and industry ratios to determine how much discretionary cash flow might be available for repayment in the event of a stress on cash flow.

Most of this they will compare to your industry standards. If you're performing in the top quartile, you're in pretty good shape. If you're in the middle half, a lot is going to depend upon where your company is on that spectrum and upon your performance trend. If you're in the lower quartile, additional support for the credit may be required, or the bank could just outright decline the loan.

In reviewing your Cash Flow history, they will look at whether or not the company was able to maintain or grow cash within the company. As we mentioned in an earlier chapter "Cash is King," they will be looking at cash position (Liquidity) and trend as it relates to sales, expense management, margin trends, debt positions, and owner withdraws.

The three primary cash flow ratios involve liquidity and debt service coverage. Most banks use the following ratios, but will use a number of others as well, in order to gain different perspectives on organizational performance.

QUICK RATIO (QR)

This Liquidity Ratio provides a measure of a company's ability to meet its short-term obligations with its liquid assets. It uses assets that can be quickly converted to cash compared to the company's current liabilities. (Obligations payable to creditors within one year.) Note that it does not include Operating Expenses. The Ratio is calculated in one of 2 methods, as follows:

$$QR = CE+MS+AR \ / \ CL$$
$$or$$
$$QR = CA\text{-}I\text{-}PE \ / \ CL$$

(QR = Quick Ratio, CE = Cash Equivalents, MS = Marketable Securities, AR = Account Receivables, CL = Current Liabilities, CA = Current Assets, I = Inventory, PE = Prepaid Expenses)

A result of '1' is considered to be normal for most companies. If it is less than 1, the company may not be able to pay off its current liabilities in the short term. Any result greater than 1 indicates that the company can easily meet its current liabilities. The higher it is above 1 the greater the flexibility as a company enters tough times.

CURRENT RATIO (CR)

The CR is a slower version of the quick ratio. It allows for all Current Assets (those that can be converted to cash within one year) to be applied to the Current Liabilities. The interpretation of the ratio is essentially the same, however, it doesn't just look at the immediate situation, but rather looks at how well the company can satisfy current liabilities over the next 12 months. If the ratio is less than '1,' it indicates that the company debts due within one year are greater than the value of assets that can be converted to cash within one year. The ratio is as follows:

$$Current\ Ratio = Current\ Assets\ /\ Current\ Liabilities$$

If the ratio is, say '3.0' it indicates that the company can cover its current liabilities three times. If this number is significantly high, it may also indicate that the company is not using its current assets efficiently.

DEBT SERVICE COVERAGE (DSC) RATIO

The DSC ratio is a measure of a company's ability to comfortably satisfy all debt payments due within one year with its annual cash flow. It effectively uses an adjusted Net Operating Income (NOI) to account for non-cash expenses that are embedded in the Income Statement. The formula is as follows:

$$DSC = EBITDA\ /\ Total\ Debt\ Service$$

(DSC = Debt Service Coverage; EBITDA = Earnings before Interest, Taxes, Depreciation, & Amortization expenses; Total Debt Service = All payment of Interest and Principal due within in one year)

This is the most utilized ratio by banks for business lending. It provides a quick perspective of the company's ability to repay debt. Typically, the minimum DSC ratio on a business loan transaction is 1.20, meaning that the company will generate $1.20 in cash flow to service each $1.00 in debt payments for the year.

There are numerous ratios and metrics used by banks to measure liquidity and cash flow. They will even vary by industry, but these three are incorporated into virtually every business analysis completed.

Once banks have become comfortable with the cash flow of the company, they'll look at your Income Statement(s) for profitability position and trend. Remember, the "Income Statement is Queen," and that's where we get profitability. As we mentioned in the section on Capital, your earnings contribute to, or detract from, the amount of capital you have to support the organization. Even if the company has positive cash flow, if they are also experiencing loss years, they are cannibalizing their capital position and essentially deteriorating their safety net. Therefore, as banks analyze profitability, they look at the position and trend of profit margins and return ratios.

These include the Gross Profit Margin (GPM), Net Profit Margin (NPM), Return on Assets (ROA) and Return on Equity (ROE). These ratios are the easiest way for the bank, or the owner, to tell if the company is generating a healthy profit. These ratios can uncover areas where your company performance needs some work, and they help narrow down where the issues reside. An explanation of each is provided below:

GROSS PROFIT MARGIN (GPM)

GPM measures how much revenue a company has left after they pay for their production costs known as, Cost of Goods Sold. (Revenue − Cost of Goods Sold = Gross Profit) The calculation is as follows:

$$GPM = Gross\ Profit\ /\ Revenue\ (Net\ Sales)$$

The higher the result of this calculation, the more you have left to cover the operating expenses of the company. When this ratio is compared to your industry standards, it shows you whether or not you need to look further into either the numerator or the denominator. If the ratio is high compared to your industry, you're either getting more revenue per sale or producing your goods and services at a lower cost. If the ratio is low, it would be wise to investigate why your revenue per sale is lagging or why your production costs are higher.

It's important to note that looking just at the result only tells part of the story. Ideally, you have the ability to see this ratio over time. A trend can add a lot to the interpretation of the results.

74

NET PROFIT MARGIN (NPM)

This may be the most important profitability measure used by the bank or the business. This ratio indicates how much of your revenue actually makes it through to profit. In essence, it measures the percent of revenue retained after all Cost of Goods Sold, Operating Expenses, and Non-Operating Expenses are paid. The calculation is as follows:

$$NPM = Net\ Income\ /\ Revenue\ (Net\ Sales)$$

The higher the result, the better for the company and the bank. However, as stated above, you must look at this result in the context of your industry performance and as a trend over time to really get the full perspective.

RETURN ON ASSETS (ROA)

This measurement is all about efficiency and indicates how well your company is using the assets at its disposal to improve bottom line profit. Again, there are a number of variations to how this can be calculated, but here is the simplest version.

$$Return\ on\ Assets\ (ROA) = Net\ Income\ /\ Total\ Assets$$

Bankers use this, and its trend, to determine the benchmark for future asset utilization and to compare the performance of your company with that of others within your industry. The final profitability ratio we'll present for measuring the degree of profitability is the Return on Equity (ROE) ratio.

RETURN ON EQUITY (ROE)

This measure informs the bank how well a company is managing the shareholder investments, owners' contributions, or retained earnings. It's an indication of Return on Investment (ROI). This helps banks evaluate the effectiveness of company management and their stewardship over the equity capital of the company. The formula is similar to Return on Assets.

Return on Equity (ROE) = Net Income / Equity (Net Worth)

Every company should be focused on profitability, and these ratios help banks determine how focused or effective they are. When taken in consideration of their position, trend, and industry comparison, they provide a valuable perspective into the potential risk level for providing the requested financing.

The final ratios we will present are those associated with the leverage position of the company. Leverage is a representation of the level of debt in the company as compared to the assets and equity of the company. Companies with high leverage have little room to maneuver during difficult times and are very dependent on credit in order to operate. This makes companies more vulnerable to creditor demands during tough times. If they are highly leveraged, their options to refinance debt with other creditors are limited. Banks prefer to lend to companies with moderate to strong equity positions and resulting lower leverage.

Therefore, banks consider if a company is highly leveraged, they have a larger demand on cash flow from outside the organization. They also recognize that using additional credit to navigate through tough times is a limited, if not a non-existent, option. The dependency on operational cash flow increases significantly. There are two ratios they consider when making this assessment. We'll start with the Debt to Asset Ratio.

DEBT TO ASSET (D/A)

The D/A ratio is also known as the "Debt Ratio." It measures the solvency of a company by looking at the company's total liabilities as a percent of its assets. Essentially, it tells the user whether or not the company could pay off all its debts through the liquidation of its assets. The calculation is as follows:

Debt Ratio = Total Liabilities / Total Assets

The formula must utilize your <u>total</u> liabilities and assets, not just current (short term) debt. The result is a percentage and the lower the percentage, the better. The lower ratio implies lower risk since the company has lower overall debt. Each industry will represent different acceptable levels, but in general, a result of .50 is reasonable. This indicates that the company has twice as many assets as they have liabilities.

If the result were 1.0, the company would have to liquidate all of its assets to satisfy its debts. From the bank's perspective, the more debt, the more demand on cash and the higher the risk of being repaid. Higher ratios also indicate that the flexibility of acquiring additional debt for the company when needed is limited, as is the willingness of banks to refinance the existing debt for better terms, or with another lender.

DEBT TO EQUITY (D/E)

The final ratio we'll present is the Debt to Equity ratio. Similar to the Debt to Asset ratio, it shows the percentage of financing that comes from investors vs. creditors. It doesn't test for solvency like the D/A ratio but rather indicates how much "skin in the game" the owners have in comparison to the lenders. If the ratio is high, then the creditors have significantly more at risk than the owners. It's relatively easy to see why this would be a concern for the lenders, but it should also be of significant concern for the owners. The calculation is as follows:

Debt to Equity Ratio = Total Liabilities / Total Equity

Debt requires repayment, while equity does not. Therefore, the higher the D/E ratio, the greater demand on cash, hence the higher risk to repayment. Additionally, when creditors have more invested than the owners, they may exercise their rights more aggressively in the event of troubled times in order to protect their investment and repayment. If the ratio is .5, each party has an equal contribution. As the result increases, the creditors are carrying more risk.

I realize that in this section on Capacity we presented a lot of numbers and formulas, but it is necessary that businesses and bankers understand why they are used, as much as how they are used.

Since Capacity is all about the ability to repay, there are a couple of other perspectives we need to review. In many businesses, the owner(s) withdraw all, or most, of the profit each year. Depending upon the business structure, this may be necessary to pay business taxes that are reported on their personal tax return. However, withdrawals in excess of taxes deplete the equity and cash reserves of the business. This can cause significant concerns for lenders.

If the owners deplete the equity and cash reserves of the business, they significantly increase the risk of default. It is especially concerning if the owners utilize the withdrawals for living expenses. When this happens, they are no longer available to be put back in the business. Even if the owner(s) invest the withdrawals in their personal investment accounts, the funds are not immediately available for use in the business, AND the business owner(s) must be willing to return cash to the business when needed.

There's nothing wrong with owners taking withdrawals. After all, it is their business. However, when this is done at a level that detrimentally increases risk in the business, they must be willing to return capital, as necessary. If they are not willing or able to do so, they should not expect a lender to provide additional funds either. Therefore, a word of caution: make sure any withdrawals are done strategically with a balance of current and future needs of the company and the owner(s).

The other point of note is in regard to Contingency Planning and Course Correction Strategies. It helps the lender get comfortable with the repayment risk associated with your business if you have already thought through the "What if" scenarios. By taking into consideration the typical negative impacts your business could encounter and developing a Contingency Plan in advance, you position the business to minimize the impact and successfully manage through tough times. Create a Contingency Plan for the top two or three potential negative circumstances - say, a recession that decreases revenue by 5, 10, or 15%, or an increase in major supply costs by 5 to 10%, etc. By projecting these impacts and developing Course Correction Strategies you minimize or eliminate repayment risk. Developing Contingency Plans is not terribly difficult. It reduces your stress about the future, exhibits strong management skills, and helps put your banker at ease. That's a pretty good return on investment.

CAPITAL

In the simplest form, from the Five Cs of Credit perspective, the bank wants to know how much money (capital) the business will be contributing to the project or acquisition being funded. Depending upon the type of request, this could range from 5-50%. On average, it's probably around 15-20%. It's all about who is going to take what level of risk. You'll need to have some "skin in the game" to acquire the funding necessary. But from a larger perspective, Capital levels in your business represent a significant criterion in the loan decision process.

The term "Capital" is one of the most broadly used terms in finance. As you recall, we covered types of capital earlier as we discussed access to cash at various points in the business life cycle. If you look the term up in the dictionary, you'll probably find no less than 4 different versions of the term. Suffice it to say, in general, they will refer to the cash, assets, or net assets that you own. In our previous representation, it focused on types of cash potentially available throughout the business life cycle.

In the Five Cs of credit, it focuses on the Net Worth or Equity (total assets minus total liabilities) that you have in your business. Essentially, what you have less what you owe. The Net Worth or Equity shown on your company Balance Sheet incorporates the Original Owner Contribution, Subsequent Owner Contributions, and the Accumulated "Net" Earnings of the company since its inception. Net Earnings is a representation of all profits earned by the company less any distributions or dividends paid out to owners.

Since Net Worth is also a function of Assets minus Liabilities, it represents the remaining investment you (the owners) have in the business. In essence, it's your overall "skin in the game." Why is that important? Lenders are being asked to take a risk with the depositor's money, and they want to know that the owner is willing to take a risk as well. If the owner has minimal Net Worth because they've taken all the profits out of the business, but want the bank to provide the cash for operations, asset acquisitions, or expansion, they're essentially asking the bank to take all the risk. Why would the bank do that when their returns are limited to the interest they collect vs. the unlimited returns available to the owners?

The level of capital in your business measures your dedication to the business or how much you believe in the risk you're taking. It also represents your ability to weather financial losses incurred during tough times or unforeseen circumstances. If you have minimal Net Worth or Equity in your business, and it is consumed through operating losses, you may soon find yourself insolvent (more liabilities than assets) or at least heavily dependent upon the lender to provide necessary capital (cash) to maintain operations. I can assure you, that's not where you want to be with your business.

So, what's the right level of capital for your business? Well, it depends. Every industry has inherent risks and therefore operate with different levels of Capital. It's important that you understand what the standard capital position is for businesses within your industry. That's a great starting benchmark. The need for capital in your particular business may be higher or lower depending on your particular circumstances. Suffice it to say, more is better.

You can access industry financial information through a variety of business information services. These services can be located by searching, "industry financial information" on the internet. Most of these services will likely have a nominal fee to obtain the information. Colleges and Universities also provide access to this type of information.

Bankers will look at your net worth from the perspective of leverage. That is, how much have you have invested in relation to others. It's a measurement of risk and commitment. The calculation is simply, total liabilities divided by total net worth. Here's a quick example:

Total Assets	$5,000,000
Total Liabilities	($3,500,000)
Total Net Worth	$1,500,000

Debt to Net Worth Ratio = $3,500,000/$1,500,000 = 2.33

In this example the banker can see that the company has $2.33 in debt for every $1.00 in Net Worth or Equity. Is that good or bad? As mentioned above, it depends. From this formula, the bank can also see that the borrower has a 30% investment in the business ($1,500,000/$5,000,000) and the creditors have a 70% investment. If the business needs to maintain a 20% equity position for safe operations, they have 10% ($500,000) that could be utilized to support potential losses while maintaining a stable financial position. Knowing this, the business and the bank can make assumptions regarding how long the business could sustain safe operations given different levels of loss.

As you can see, both the level of Capital contribution by the owner on any given loan transaction and the level of Capital (Net Worth) maintained by the business are important in determining a business's access to bank lending. It's ok if the business owner has operated with a practice of withdrawing virtually all profits out of the business and leaves the business balance sheet with minimal Capital. Bankers get it - the owner went into business to reap the benefits of the profits and therefore is entitled to receive those whenever they're available. However, if they do that, when it comes to borrowing, the owner needs to be prepared to pledge or contribute personal financial assets to mitigate the risk assessed by the lender. If they're not willing, their ability to be approved for loans may be impaired.

COLLATERAL

When lending money, banks predominately focus on the cash flow of the business being adequate to service all debt requirements with a certain degree of cushion. We covered that in detail in the section on "Capacity." Now, we're going to provide some insight on "Collateral." Collateral is defined by the assets you pledge to additionally support the repayment of your loan.

Banks look to take conditional rights to ownership of assets as a backup repayment source to be utilized if the business fails to repay the loan. Those collateralized assets provide security to the bank that it will recover the depositors' money that was lent to the borrower.

As an example, when you borrow money to purchase your office building, the bank typically takes the building as collateral by filing a mortgage on the property. That mortgage gives them the right to take ownership of the property should the business fail to pay the loan as agreed. If that happens, the bank sells the asset and uses the proceeds from the sale to repay the loan. The same can be said for a variety of other business and personal assets used as collateral in support of obtaining a loan.

How much and what specific collateral are required to support your loan request will depend upon the request itself, the lenders preference, what assets are available, and the potential liquidation value of those assets. Most lenders pre-determine how much they are willing to lend on the standard types of collateral. This is called their advance rate. Here are some typical business asset loan advance rates applied to market or liquidation values. Please recognize that these can vary widely due to markets, circumstances, condition of assets, marketability, etc.

Commercial Real Estate	80%
Equipment – New	70%
Equipment – Used	50%
Inventory – Monitored	70%
Accounts Receivable – Monitored	80%

A "Blanket Lien" may also be used by banks to secure the repayment of the loan. A Blanket Lien essentially pledges all the assets of the business to the bank as opposed to using some specific assets while not pledging others.

While not technically considered collateral, it's appropriate that we discuss "Guarantees" in this section. Lenders may require a personal guarantee as additional support for a business loan. In essence, as the business owner, you personally guarantee to repay the loan in the event that the business is unable to do so. The guarantor could be someone other than the business owner, but the agreement is the same. The guarantee may, or may not, need to be further secured with personal assets.

The request by banks for collateral and/or guarantees all center around the need for them to minimize the risk of loss in their fiduciary responsibility to the depositors of the bank. Before applying for a loan, you should be aware of what assets you have to offer for collateral, which ones you're willing to pledge, whether or not you're willing to provide a blanket lien, and/or a personal guarantee.

The requests from the bank and your willingness to pledge assets or guarantee the loan will all affect the likelihood of obtaining the loan. This is probably the most customized portion of any business loan structure.

CONDITIONS

As the lender gains comfort with the character of the applicant, they begin to assess the Conditions under which the loan would be provided. There are several factors the lender will consider. Some of them are within your control, while others are not. The lender's intent in reviewing the conditions relevant to the request is to determine the potential risk associated with loan repayment.

1.) **Purpose & Structure of the Loan** – Before any other assessment makes sense, the lender needs to understand the purpose and structure of the loan. Conventional purposes would include working capital, equipment or inventory purchases, and real estate acquisition or rehabilitation; however, there are numerous other requests that bankers see. What they're looking for is the logic behind the request. Does it align with the normal business operations? Does the applicant have the knowledge and experience to manage the use of funds and the repayment source?

They're considering the ability of the bank <u>and</u> the borrower to appropriately manage the loan. For instance, some banks don't provide construction financing because they don't have the skillsets and resources with which to monitor and manage the funding process. Others may offer construction funding, but a particular applicant may not have appropriate construction experience in relation to the proposed project. If these don't align, the bank most likely won't approve the loan due to the increased risk.

They also consider if the request fits within their lending policies, is legal, or borders on unethical behavior. For instance, if a borrower wants financing to purchase and operate an old landfill, the bank may have a policy against lending to this industry because of environmental liability concerns. Maybe the request is for financing a business transaction with an individual, foreign country or a company that is on the Office of Foreign Asset Control (OFAC) Sanctions list, where the bank is prohibited from providing funds. Or the request could be interpreted to border on unethical practices or that the business has a high risk of illegal activity, such as marijuana production. While some States have legalized the production of marijuana for medicinal or recreational purposes, the bank may still be reluctant to lend due to its position on the use of marijuana in society and/or the potential for the production to find its way into illegal use, thereby creating a potential reputational or legal risk for the bank.

Loan structure is considered as well. For instance, if the request is for a 15-year vehicle loan, the bank may deem that the loan would exceed the useful life of the vehicle. The reverse could also be true. The request may be for the borrower to repay a building purchase loan within one year through the extremely optimistic cash flow projections for a new enterprise. The bank may choose not to provide the financing due to the degree of uncertainty regarding repayment.

2.) **Condition and Direction of the Business** – The bank will also consider the Condition of the business. Is it financially stable? Does it have a consistent positive earnings history? Is the financial performance trend positive, negative, or erratic? Other conditions may also be considered. Such as, is the management team capable and stable? Are there near-term ownership or management changes planned? Are the facility, equipment, and production systems viable over the term of the loan? The review of business conditions is focused on things within the business owner's control.

3.) **External Conditions** – We are all too aware of how external factors can affect our business even though these conditions are out of our control. As the lender considers these external conditions, they're thinking about the likelihood that they would negatively impact the borrower's ability to repay and the borrower's ability to survive through these Conditions. The bank will look at the following types of external conditions:

   a. **Competitive Environment** – They're going to consider how competitive your industry is, and where your company is ranked within that competitive space. Take, for instance, craft breweries. Ten years ago, it was a novel and unique approach to the brewing industry. Today, as I write this, there are about 10 craft breweries within a 20 minute drive from my home. As craft breweries proved their ability to prosper, it was easy to be comfortable lending into the competitive environment. Today, one has to consider how effective the applicant will be securing shelf space within grocery and liquor stores or tap space within bars and restaurants.

   b. **Industry Conditions** – It seems obvious that the bank would consider the state of the industry in which the business resides. As business cycles occur, every industry goes through good times and bad, as well as evolution and maturation. Banks will look to understand how your industry is performing and try to determine if there are any impending issues that could affect future viability for your company. Let's look at a few examples.

   The Hospitality, Restaurant, and Travel industries were significantly impacted by the 2020 pandemic.

While these impacts are outside the borrower's control, they present significant risks associated with repayment of loans and/or business survival. Other industry impacts can come from industries outside of the one in which you do business. What if your business is in Shipping and Logistics, and due to global events oil prices double, thereby impacting your fuel costs? With the exception of personnel cost, fuel is likely the largest operating expense in your company. Absorbing this cost will dramatically decrease profit margins and your capacity to service debt.

c. **Economic & Regulatory Conditions** - Businesses are obviously affected by economic conditions, but the impacts of those conditions are not evenly distributed across all businesses. Therefore, banks look at how businesses performed through previous recessionary and growth periods to assist in determining how well a business may perform through future downturns or economic expansions.

The regulatory environment clearly has an impact on businesses as well. Laws and regulations can dramatically help or hinder business performance and risk. Consider the impact on the coal industry. Regulations imposed on this industry, coupled with new competing energy sources subsidized with state and federal funds, caused significant impacts to this sector of the energy industry.

We previously referenced the impact on restaurants due to the pandemic. Well, the pandemic itself didn't necessarily create those impacts. The vast majority of the impact was generated through laws enacted to limit their occupancy, hours of business, or requirements to close, in an effort to keep people safe from infection.

These are just a few examples on how political and legal actions can affect the performance and risk of businesses. It's not about whether you agree with these actions or not, they unpredictably occur in various forms and at various times, and businesses need to position themselves with every avenue possible to allow them to survive.

The final type of economic/political condition that can materially affect businesses is that of confidence and uncertainty. If the general public feels confident that the foreseeable future is positive and beneficial to their financial health, businesses will benefit from more robust purchasing. If, however, the public is uncertain about the future and concerned for their financial wellbeing they will, in their own self-interest, slow their purchases and reserve what cash they have.

Well, we've covered the Five Cs of Credit. Hopefully, they have helped both the business owners and bankers have a better understanding of how they should be applied. A deeper understanding of these five characteristics of lending will make for a much more successful borrower/lender relationship.

CHAPTER 11
SUSTAINABLE GROWTH RATE (SGR)

As we move on from the Five Cs of Credit, I want to present one more calculation of which bankers and business owners should be aware. The Sustainable Growth Rate is one of the most valuable, yet underutilized calculations regarding business performance. Bankers seldom use it or understand it and business owners either don't know it exists or haven't seen the value in using it in the management of their business.

I first encountered this early in my career and once I understood what it could tell me about a business, I began relying on it as one of the calculations used in underwriting business loan opportunities. It has proven to be surprisingly insightful. The calculation is as follows:

$$SGR = Return\ on\ Equity\ (ROE) \times (1 - Dividend\ Payout\ Ratio)$$

We previously discussed Return on Equity, and the Dividend Payout Ratio is the percentage of earnings paid to the owners as dividends or withdrawals. Using this calculation assumes that your company wants to maintain a target capital structure.

The Sustainable Growth Rate tells us the maximum rate of growth that a company can sustain without having to finance growth with additional debt or equity. For a company to achieve its maximum growth rate, it must maximize sales efforts, focus on high margin products, and manage inventory, accounts payable, and accounts receivable well.

Therefore, a company that has a sustainable growth rate of 14% but the company desires to grow at a rate of 18% won't be able to achieve it using their current plans and policies. Knowing this helps management recognize the potential need for appropriate operational changes. Additionally, they will likely need to raise more capital, reduce dividends, or both to achieve their 18% growth goal.

On the other hand, if a company has an SGR of 9%, but is growing at a rate of 5%, they should have internal resources with which they can finance additional growth or increase its dividend. If they want to grow beyond their SGR of 9%, they will need additional financing. Understanding this calculation helps bankers understand the effectiveness of management and/or the need for additional financing. Monitoring the difference between the SGR and actual or expected growth rate also allows management and bankers to anticipate the challenges or opportunities that may be encountered by the business going forward.

The ability for a company to maintain its SGR can be difficult. When companies experience a decline in their SGR it may be caused by a number or factors. These include compressed profit margins, competition, market saturation for their product or service, poor long term planning, or economic conditions.

As we discussed in the business life cycle, companies increase revenue throughout the Growth Phase. Eventually they may reach a point of sales saturation with its products. This is likely to indicate the beginning of the Decline or Mature Phase. Reinvestment will be needed to regain the expected growth rate. Expansion into new or other products, new markets, sales methods etc., could all reduce profit margins. Lower margins mean lower profitability, a strain on financial resources, and the need for additional capital. But if they don't reinvest, they risk stagnation or elimination.

As you can see, understanding the SGR and actual growth rates of a company provides for a great perspective on the future prospects of a company, leading to proactive decisions regarding operations, dividends, and capital.

CHAPTER 12

DON'T BE STUPID! – MANAGING
THE BANKING RELATIONSHIP

Bankability has a lot to do with relationship management, and quality relationships are built on trust. Throughout this book, I have attempted to provide business owners and bankers a perspective on the lender/borrower relationship that leads to a more bankable business for both. In the last few chapters, I will provide some tips that will complement the previous bankability discussions. In this chapter, "Don't Be Stupid!," I provide insight to real events where business owners and bankers have let their self-importance get in front of their business sense. These self-inflicted wounds cause more damage to a productive business relationship than any of the previous information I've provided. You'd be amazed at what I've seen. Here are a few examples:

> **Spending Money to Reduce or Avoid Taxes** – I can't count the times when explaining an operating loss that a business owner has told me, "I spent the money so I wouldn't have to pay taxes." Here's the problem. If you spent the money on something you didn't really need, or for something you would eventually need but not now, you may have done

more harm than good. If it's something you need and will utilize in the short term, it makes sense. But if not, all you've really done is trade assets. Cash for something else. If the purchased assets depreciate or are not put to use generating revenue or reducing cost, you've harmed the company's efficiency, profitability, and reputation to save a few tax dollars. Remember, profitable companies pay taxes, unprofitable ones don't. Be cautious about using this strategy and make sure it has the right return on investment. If it consistently creates a loss or significant impairment to margins, it will call into question management's intent.

Keeping Secrets by Limiting Access to Information –
Refusing to provide information to the banker, for whatever reason, is a poor approach. Any time this happens the banker will assume the worst and that you're trying to hide something that would be detrimental to the transaction. Typically, it's something like your personal investment account statements. Borrowers don't want the lender expecting them to inject additional cash or ask for the account as additional collateral, so they refuse to provide it. If you, as a borrower, don't want to inject additional cash or pledge the investment account, simply provide the information, then say so. The banker may only be wanting to validate cash available for future support of the company. Why jeopardize your reputation and trust by keeping secrets?

And Bankers, don't ask for what you don't need. Asking for more information just to check the box and show that it's in the file isn't fair to the borrower. Get the information you need to appropriately support your decision and move on. Asking for the sake of asking doesn't necessarily make you or the transaction any better.

Limiting or Avoiding Communication – This is one of
the worst things a borrower or a banker can do in a banking relationship. When the borrower and banker don't communicate, it's perceived as, "all is well, and I don't need to worry about it" by both parties. That sounds pretty good, until all is not well. It's a problem when the bank decides to

change policies or not renew a line of credit and waits to the last minute to tell the borrower because they'd rather not be the bearer of bad news. And it never helps when a borrower knows they are going to default one of their loan covenants, but doesn't say anything hoping the banker won't see it. All we've done in these situations is break each other's trust and create a bigger problem. Develop a regular and consistent communication process to share both good and bad news.

Adding Loan Covenants to "Strengthen the Deal" – Loan covenants are a key component to business loans that benefit the bank and the borrower. They are essentially additional agreements to the standard terms of the loan documents. They are customized for each borrower or situation and assist the bank in managing the credit risk associated with any borrower or transaction. They generally come in three forms: financial performance, reporting requirements, or specific expected future events. For example, a financial performance covenant might be that the business needs to have a debt service coverage ratio of 1.20 at each year end. A reporting requirement covenant might require the borrower to provide financial statements to the bank within 30 days of each calendar quarter end. A future event covenant would require the borrower to do something in the future, such as inject additional capital.

These covenants allow the bank to monitor the risk associated with ongoing business operations. Businesses should recognize that these same requirements help them identify risk as well, and by doing so, help management implement appropriate course corrections in conjunction with the bank. While they typically aren't perceived as such, they're really a win-win for both parties.

Covenants should not be taken lightly by the borrower or the lender and should not be onerously or inappropriately applied to any loan transaction. Sometimes, bankers add covenants to a deal in order to try and "win" approvals from their loan committees or supervisors. Their thinking is that if they structure enough monitoring of the credit and borrower, it'll look safer to the decision maker. Sometimes, even decision makers do this to try and justify their approval of the credit. This is foolish gamesmanship. Covenants do not necessarily make the loan a better loan. The sole purpose of covenants is to monitor or address key risk areas in the transaction.

With the appropriate covenants, bankers and borrowers can discuss negative events before they become catastrophic to develop appropriate course correction strategies. That's it. They don't make your business or the loan transaction better. But they should make the management of the business and the credit better. More covenants are not necessarily an improvement. Use them as needed, and stop.

Agree to Something You Can't or Won't Do – This goes both ways. I've had borrowers agree to do things that they never intended to do and once their loan was funded just ignored their responsibility hoping it wouldn't make a difference. Unfortunately, once uncovered, their deception had already done significant damage, whether or not complying with the agreement would have mattered.

Bankers can have the same problem. Let's say they request the covenants previously described. If they require a quarterly Debt Service Coverage covenant test, but after receiving the quarterly financial statements, never test it, then why have it? If you're asking for monthly reporting but don't look at it, stop asking for it. If this loan approval implies that you'll approve the next loan, don't allow the assumption to remain. Be clear about future actions.

Going it Alone to the Point of Failure – I hate it when this happens. A borrower obtains a loan for their business and everything is progressing well. Then something unfortunate happens. They lose their largest customer, or a key employee, worse yet, a team. Maybe sales have just slowed due to new competition or market changes. In any event, the borrower keeps trying to make it work and doesn't ask for help. None of us are successful on our own. We all rely upon others for our success. When challenges occur, reach out for help. Your banker may not be a bad source of information or potential solutions. They can't tell you what to do - it's your business - but they can share perspectives and solutions they've seen others use successfully. Get help from others as well, but start with your banker. Your bank has a vested interest in your success.

Selling Assets Secured by the Lender – If this is done without lender consent, it's called fraud, and defrauding a federally insured financial institution is a federal crime. You really don't want to be this stupid. Even if it's not intentional to defraud the lender, get permission first. If you don't, at best, you'll have significantly damaged your banking relationship. And, at worst, you'll go to jail. Unfortunately, I know. I can count at least 5 previous borrowers over my 35 years in banking that ended up in prison for pulling a stunt like this.

Purchasing Assets Before the Funds are Available – Don't assume your lender is going to provide the funding you need to purchase an asset. Get your loan approval first. Even a verbal, or conditional approval, prior to purchase is better than none at all. To do this on the assumption you'll get funded is arrogant to the extreme. Remember, it's not your money you're borrowing, it's your neighbors'.

Lie! – I probably should have discussed this one first. Unfortunately, it's probably the most prevalent of stupid actions. Not only does it seriously violate the Character component of the Five Cs of Credit, but it's also not sustainable. Eventually it gets found out, and there's no going back. Don't hedge your bets or paint the most favorable picture. Be brutally honest and deal with it.

Wait for the Lender to Call – This goes back to proactive communication. If you happen to have a banker that hasn't yet learned the value of proactive communication, take the lead, and reach out to them. Force them to put you on their calendar for regular meetings. Avoiding communication and assuming everything's ok is a bad strategy. Why should you be the one to reach out, you ask? It's your business just as much as it's their loan. You both have a responsibility here. Don't allow both to fail to talk, just because one does.

Pretend You Didn't Know – How often have I heard, "But I didn't realize that was in the loan documents, or that I pledged those assets." This statement, whether true or not speaks to the quality of management and the integrity of the borrower. When you borrow money, you're responsible for understanding the terms and conditions under which you borrowed it. Read the documents. If you don't understand them, ask questions.

If the lender can't explain it, ask your attorney, or find another lender. When I started in banking, before I was allowed to lend any money, one of the things I was required to do was read and understand all the loan documents that I was asking the borrower to sign. Your lender should be prepared to review and explain everything in your loan documents. Don't sign something to save time, take the time to read it and understand it.

Demand Something Without Explanation – This typically is the failure of the banker. Sometimes as the borrower/lender relationship evolves, the lender begins asking for more or different information, collateral, covenants, and/or terms in the agreement. They may assume these to be logical requests without need for explanation. In this case, lenders need to remember the problem with assuming things. If the borrower doesn't understand the reasoning behind your request, why wouldn't they just choose to do business with another lender that doesn't request so much? By providing an explanation of your requests, you educate your borrower on the risk management approach to borrowing that benefits their business as well as the bank. If you don't understand the benefit to the borrower, go find it. The reason for the request is not, "Because my bank said so" and the benefit isn't always, "So you can get the loan."

If your lender didn't explain the changes, ask them to. Knowing why the lender is requesting something will provide you with a better understanding of their perspective. This in turn will assist you in managing your bankability.

Blame the Lender – Inevitably something goes wrong. I've been amazed at how often the borrower, or the media, immediately blames the lender. I'm not saying that there aren't times when the lender does something in their interest that negatively affects the borrower, but it's counter-intuitive to their overall objective of having a banking relationship with a well performing borrower such that it ensures repayment.

It's typically only when borrower performance has significantly deteriorated that the bank starts to act in their own self-interest, making it appear as if it's the bank's fault. Banks don't cause poor borrower performance or position themselves to have poor performing loans any more than a business would position itself to sell products or services to customers that couldn't pay. When you feel like blaming the lender, dig a little deeper. The cause of the problem is likely elsewhere.

I feel compelled here to offer a word of caution. There is such a thing as predatory lending. Predatory lenders entice people to borrow under terms and conditions that perpetuate the borrower's failure to pay in order to gain exorbitant interest rates or access to collateral pledged. This type of lending is a violation of law and avoided by virtually all banks. Their business model is to assist and do business with successful borrowers. They lose money when things go wrong, and the reputational risk of predatory lending is too high. If you question the motives of the lender at the beginning of the relationship, for your own sake, move on to another lending source.

Act Like You're Entitled – This goes both ways. Lenders, you are not entitled to make the loan, and borrowers, you're not entitled to receive it. We both have to earn the right to do business with each other. In business lending, banks, for the most part, can choose which businesses to lend to, understanding that competition forces them to provide fair and competitive terms across a broad market. That being said, just because you're in business, doesn't mean that you're qualified as a borrower at all lending institutions. Lending and borrowing money are privileges. In many respects that's why it needs to be a relationship, rather than a transaction.

Steal or Hide Assets – Once a borrower resorts to this, it's all over but the shouting. I've always been flabbergasted when this occurs. What does anyone hope to gain with this type of behavior? All it does is exacerbate the problems. As a borrower, if it has gotten to this point, "Toughen up and deal with it." Quit playing games. This type of action will only damage your opportunity to rebound in the future.

These are simply some of the things I've seen over time that damage the borrower/lender relationship and don't provide value to the bank or the business. Several of these are driven by emotional reactions to various circumstances. Try to keep the emotion out of decision making when things get difficult, and work towards a strong relationship with your borrower or banker. In the long run this will serve your purposes well.

CHAPTER 13
KEY TIPS FOR SURVIVAL AND SUCCESS

As we mentioned before, there are three major reasons for business failure or success. Those are Market, Team, and Capital. There's a lot that goes into each of those components, so let me layout a framework for ensuring that your business not only survives, but succeeds. These tips come from watching businesses do just that in good times and bad.

Know Your Marketplace – This may seem intuitive, but do you really understand who is interested in buying your product or service, or more importantly, why they buy it? The clear alignment between the marketplace and what you provide is critical. If you're off target here, you'll always struggle to grow sales. In addition, you must know your competition and what differentiates you and your product or service from them. Once you know that, revisit the 'who' would buy from me and 'why.' Write this information down and refer to it throughout the evolution of your company.

Maintain a Clear Vision – Knowing what you want your company to look like in 3 – 5 years and what it will take to get it there will guide you through all the unforeseen circumstances you'll encounter along the way. Most businesspeople can give you a general description of their future, but few can do so in detail. And, even fewer can tell you the specific requirements for getting there. Develop your vision, share it with others, refine it at every opportunity and identify what it will take to get there. A strong comprehensive annual Strategic Planning process will keep your vision alive and your progress strong.

Plan to Succeed – Your Strategic Plan and Business Plans should be interconnected. If they don't entirely support each other, they're just wishful stories. Implementing a Strategic Plan consumes resources. Make sure you have the resources to achieve the Objectives, Goals, and Strategies outlined in your plan. Your Business Plans should have strong monitoring processes in the form of easily readable dashboards that focus on metrics indicating progress on plan. Your management meetings should be designed for the reporting and course correction discussions necessary to achieve your plans.

As they say, "A failure to plan, is a plan to fail." Use this simple approach to ensuring that your plan remains active. Plan, Execute, Evaluate, Repeat (PEER). Use this approach throughout your daily processes with a focus on the plan, and you'll accelerate your success.

Set Goals – If I don't have a target, I could hit anything, or nothing for that matter, and call it success. Sounds pretty foolish, doesn't it? But have you really set Goals, or do you just kind of have an end in mind? When setting goals, make them SMART goals. That is, Specific, Measurable, Attainable, Relevant, and Time Bound. Without an anticipated destination, you'll never know if you've arrived nor when you need to course correct.

Build the Right Team – Having the right team, both internal and external to the organization, can make all the difference in success and survival. Most companies are really good at writing job descriptions that detail the functions of any given position. But I would suggest another approach. If you know what needs to be done to achieve your vision and goals, try identifying the skill sets needed before worrying about the actual functions a position will perform. Hiring for skill sets first will always prove beneficial. Let's use sales as an example. You could interview and hire a lot of people capable of performing the actual functions in the sales process, phone calls, prospect visits, presentations, closing paperwork, etc., but if they are not skilled at sales, they will be less than successful. Start with skills and build the right team. As circumstances and needs evolve, re-assess the team, and make changes, as necessary.

Get Organized & Stay Focused – When you're the owner of the business, a lot of stuff comes your way. It's easy to get distracted and prioritize the issue of the moment. The key to success here is to organize your priorities in advance; then, as issues arise, determine who else on the team can handle them. This not only develops your team for future responsibilities, it allows you to focus on your priorities. Give your priorities dedicated time on your calendar and zealously protect those times. If necessary, use the Urgent and Important grid to help you stay in the appropriate quadrant.

Implement the Right Tools – When you and your team are focused on the objectives, you will be able to identify tools that will help you achieve them. Take, for instance, how a CRM (Client Relationship Management) system can add to your sales and customer service team's efficiency and effectiveness. Would Project Management software help accelerate the completion of key projects? Maybe engaging a third-party Lead Generation or Marketing Team would prove beneficial. Whatever the tools that help you succeed, get and use them.

Never Stop Learning – Even once your business is up and running, don't stop learning about new products, services, markets, and ways of doing things. Once you stop, the business will stagnate. Invite challenges and look for creative solutions. Admit it when you need help and go find it. Remember, you're leading the organization. If you're stuck in a rut, so is the organization.

Work "On" More Than "In" Your Business – I know we've all heard this before, but it's worth repeating. Only after you've built quite an effective team will you be able to spend virtually all your time working "On" the business. In smaller organizations, the owner will always have a certain amount of time committed to working "In" the business. But as your business grows, make sure you build the team to take on more responsibility, allowing you to stay focused working "On" your business. This is when you'll see things accelerate.

Work "Smart" and "Hard" – Neither success nor survival will show up just because you want them to. You need to work "Smart" so that you don't waste time on things that don't make much difference. But, at the same time, you'll need to work "Hard" and put in some long hours. Working "Smart" isn't necessarily easy and working "Hard" isn't without merit. It takes both to survive and be successful. Ask any successful business owner.

Take Ownership – My last tip for business survival and success is, "Take Ownership." This is your company. You started it, you wanted it, you own it. When things go well celebrate those successes with your team, and when things go wrong, take ownership for failing to get the right resources to effectively achieve the objective. Always keep a positive perspective and share a realistic but optimistic outlook. The results won't always be positive, but your proposed solutions and course corrections can provide a positive perspective on the future. Your success and survival aren't all about you, but you need to own up to the results and carry on. Blame doesn't get you anywhere because you believe it's someone else's problem. Take on the problems head on. Get them solved and keep moving.

Hopefully, these tips have provided you with some guidance and direction to help your company succeed and survive in good times and bad. Should your business experience tough times be sure and do these four things:

1. **Grow Revenue Aggressively.** Put at least as much effort into growing revenue as you do in cutting expenses, maybe even more aggressive. Remember, in the long run, expense reduction will not grow profits.

2. **Talk With all Your Stakeholders.** This includes Investors, Customers, Suppliers, Bankers, etc. Gather as much information as you can to improve the situation.

3. **Make a New Plan.** Your old plan is likely no longer valid. Develop a new one based on the current situation. You'll need it, and your banker will likely want to see it. Don't wait for them to ask for it.

4. **Reinject Capital.** Determine how much cash you can put your hands on and divide by your monthly operating costs to find out how long you can survive without income. If necessary, reinject capital into the business to provide a cushion. If your survival time is less than 3 months, you absolutely need to inject capital. Ideally, you want 6 – 12 months of operating capital available for tough times.

CHAPTER 14
LEVERAGING THE USE
OF PROFESSIONALS

I've covered a lot of territory in regard to bankability, but in my effort to provide guidance, I purposefully didn't get into a lot of detail. I've referenced a couple of times throughout this book that business owners should seek the help of others. At times this means the help of other professionals. Business owners should never hesitate to use the experience and knowledge of their Attorneys and Accountants (CPA's). But they should also capitalize on the vast knowledge that comes from Marketing, Advertising, Sales, Operations, Human Resources, and other professionals. Not all businesses can justify having this level of expertise in house, and paying a fraction of the cost for third party services is money well spent. Trainers, Consultants, and Business Coaches can provide valuable services that will accelerate your success. Let's take a moment to differentiate some of these titles.

"Trainers" are individuals that can provide knowledge and skill training for management and staff. These individuals are assisting the business in establishing baseline or advanced knowledge across the organization. The business might provide training on the company culture, specific job functions, market knowledge, or behavioral and communication skills. Typically, there is a set syllabus that may be customized to the needs of the organization. The benefit to utilizing Trainers is that they bring with them an expertise in the knowledge and presentation of materials that allows participants to embrace and absorb the material.

Too often, when we try training in-house, we have supervisors or management speaking to staff. The participants attend out of duty rather than benefit. Additionally, they've probably heard it before and don't engage or absorb the material as well as they should. There's an old saying that "An expert needs to come from 50 miles away in order to be considered an expert." Obviously, this isn't true, but the essence is correct. When training participants hear from someone they haven't heard before and carries solid credentials, they're more apt to listen, engage, and retain the information, just because it's new.

"Consultant" is a broadly used term that could be defined as someone that, for a fee, provides expert advice to supplement the in-house knowledge of management. The key word here is "expert." Think about it this way: when you have an Information Technology (IT) problem that exceeds the knowledge and skills of your IT staff, you hire an IT consultant. If your Human Resources (HR) department needs assistance in Benefits Management, HR Policies, or Compliance you hire an HR consultant who is an expert in those particular areas.

A "Business Coach" is a newer term and carries a little more ambiguity. These individuals can bring a vast amount of value to the organization's performance. Business Coaches generally work directly, and confidentially, with the owner or Chief Executive Officer (CEO) of the company. As opposed to a consultant that applies their expertise and provides a solution for the company, Coaches work with the business leader to accelerate the business performance. As you may have heard, "It's lonely at the top." Well, it really is. I've been there. The leader of the company has few people they can discuss matters with that don't bring a significant conflict of interest.

If they discuss certain matters with their management team, they're concerned that they'll appear weak for not having the answers. In addition, the management team will likely tell them what they think they want to hear. Family and friends may not offer the level of experience or knowledge on topics and it's sometimes difficult to discuss business with family. Other business leaders can be a good source, but you may be uncomfortable sharing confidential information, or they'll respond casually because they're just sharing an opinion rather than in informed perspective.

So, a Business Coach becomes a confidential professional that listens and asks a lot of questions. They will challenge you to think through alternatives, select courses of action, develop actionable plans, hold you accountable to complete them, look for course corrections when things go wrong, review or facilitate your Strategic Planning, work with you to develop the appropriate monitoring processes, management communications, transition plans and just about anything you, as a business owner or CEO, need to prioritize to achieve success at an accelerated rate.

But how do you go about selecting a Business Coach? It's not as easy as identifying a consultant with a specific expertise, and there are a lot of people out there calling themselves Business Coaches. All of them have good management backgrounds, and it's more important that they are experienced in coaching a variety of businesses rather than experience directly in your industry, business, or even your job. What is helpful is finding a coach that has worked with a lot of businesses, seen a lot of good and bad situations, understands management principals, financial reporting and analysis, operational challenges, and team development. When a coach brings a broad and diverse background with solid experience, hire them. They're hard to find.

CHAPTER 15
WHY DIDN'T MY BANKER TELL ME THIS?

By now you might be asking yourself why your banker hasn't told you what is found in this book. And, if you're thinking my banker already explained all of this, that's great! Good job! You've found a high quality lender and likely a great business bank! There are great bankers out there that make this a key part of their client relationship management. If you don't have one, ask around. You'll find other business owners that benefit from a great banking relationship. I could write an entire book on the definition of a great banking relationship, but it starts with a lender that works with the best long term interest of the borrower as a priority.

Alternatively, there are bankers that don't provide this type of guidance. My initial thought is that it's probably not in their job description, nor part of their bank's culture. Most lenders are charged with finding new loan opportunities, not developing long term relationships. Sure, you'll find this rhetoric in their marketing material. The lenders title might actually be "Relationship Manager," but that doesn't mean they'll provide the kind of guidance we're describing here.

As the Corporate Chief Credit Officer for an $8.5B bank, I would hold regular town hall discussions with the lenders and bank management in eight offices across three states. In one such series of town hall meetings, I asked them to tell me what relationship management meant to them. Across all eight offices, I captured three distinctly different perspectives.

One group thought relationship management meant getting close to your customer and developing a personal bond. The lender would come to know personal information about the borrower's family, such as birth dates, anniversaries, favorite vacation spots, preferred recreational activities, etc. The closer they became connected with the borrower, the deeper the relationship.

Another version of relationship management sounded like something that came out of the marketing department. These lenders felt that relationship management was about, what bankers call, share of wallet. Share of wallet is a term that references the number of products and services sold to the customer. The more products and services sold, the deeper the share of wallet and hence, the deeper the relationship.

The final definition that came up was one where the relationship was managed from a mutual benefit perspective. The lender, recognizing that quality borrowers meant a well performing loan portfolio, would assist the business, through the sharing of information and insight. It was considered that this approach developed strong businesses and helped them avoid problems with their financing needs.

The reality is that true relationship management involves all three of these definitions. It was more a matter of the lenders' primary objective.

Banks position and train lenders to look for businesses that already qualify for loans. If they meet the core requirement for loan approval, there is a general assumption that the other components will be satisfactorily met as well. That assumption leads to unfortunate discoveries during the due diligence and underwriting process, causing borrower frustration when the loan is declined. Additionally, many banks compensate lenders for loan volume or share of wallet. While these may have certain loan quality parameters associated with eligible compensation, they seldom have measurements for client relationship management that improves the performance of the business.

There's a reason for this. Banks and lenders don't own your business. When bankers begin providing advice to business borrowers, it can quickly turn into, or be perceived as, requirements of the borrower to receive or maintain access to loan funds. The problem occurs when the borrowers implement the guidance provided, and it generates negative results. This can potentially cause lender liability, where the bank could be held responsible for any damage done to the business.

Lender liability was a common defense for businesses that experienced problems during the recession in the early 1980's. Given that experience, banks are reluctant to provide any guidance to business. That's one reason why lenders won't tell you some of the things in this book. That's why I wrote it.

From the banker's perspective, they might ask why the business borrower doesn't already know this. They may believe that it's the business's responsibility to be prepared prior to requesting borrowed funds. That's not necessarily true, but that's a reasonable presumption to be made. In general, even when lenders recognize the need to provide guidance on borrowing, it tends to be more procedural, structural, and requirement focused. It's not necessarily the best analogy, but it's a little like the salesperson that is busy selling the features of a product rather than the benefits. They don't get past the first tier of information to recognize the value of a deeper explanation.

All of this tends to generate bank cultures that are intrinsically more transaction focused than relationship focused. It's unfortunate because a quality working relationship with your banker can provide great mutual benefits. It is true that it's not the banker's job to run your business, but providing guidance on bankability can prove very valuable for both parties.

CONCLUSION

We've covered a lot, and I hope you've gained some perspective on how to position your company for access to cash in good times and bad. In many ways, bankability is about taking control of your business and managing your banking relationship in the most beneficial manner. Additionally, I hope you were able to take away a few actionable items that will help you grow your business. Think about bankability as a business barometer. If your company is bankable, no matter the circumstances, congratulations! That means you're running a great company. If your company isn't bankable, through good times and bad, you need to improve its performance and positioning. Call me. I know a great coach and we'll work together to get you on a solid path to success.